Crossing Guadalupe Street

Dear Jack,

Thank you so very much for your leadership & generosity. I appreciate & value your voice.

May this book introduce my family & Roots to you.

With much gratitude,

David Maldonado Jr.

11-2001

Crossing Guadalupe Street

GROWING UP HISPANIC AND PROTESTANT

David Maldonado, Jr.

UNIVERSITY OF NEW MEXICO PRESS
Albuquerque

First edition
Library of Congress Cataloging-in-Publication Data

Maldonado, David.
Crossing Guadalupe Street : growing up Hispanic and Protestant /
David Maldonado, Jr.—1st ed.
p. cm.
ISBN 0-8263-2231-X (alk. paper)
1. Maldonado, David—Childhood and youth.
2. Mexican Americans—Texas—Seguin—Biography.
3. Protestants—Texas—Seguin—Biography.
4. Mexican Americans—Texas—Seguin—Ethnic identity.
5. Seguin (Tex.)—Biography.
6. Seguin (Tex.)—Ethnic relations.
7. Seguin (Tex.)—Social life and customs—20th century.
I. Title.
F394.S43 M35 2001
976.4′34—dc21
2001001672

Contents

Preface

Writing about your life experiences can be pretentious and risky. It can be pretentious because others may not be interested. It can be risky because a life cannot be fitted within the pages of a book. Nonetheless, for the sake of telling a story that is shared by many who are Hispanic and Protestant and for the sake of telling a story that has not been told before, I accept the challenge. I do so to encourage Protestant-Catholic dialogue and mutual understanding and respect.

I am indebted to the Lilly Endowment and Southern Methodist University for their generous funding of a sabbatical that made this project possible. I thank them for their support of this and other projects. I am grateful to Mario García for reading a draft and offering helpful insights and suggestions and to Barbara Guth for her guidance in the production of this volume.

But most of all I am deeply appreciative to my wife, Charlotte, for her patience, encouragement, and support. I could not have completed this book without her. I am also deeply grateful to our sons, David III and Carlos, to our granddaughters, Maya and Rayna, and to our daughter-in-law, Kecia, for being a loving family. May they always remember our story and from whence we have come.

Introduction

This is my story of growing up Mexican-American in Texas in the 1940s and 1950s. The story takes place in a barrio of Seguin, a small south central Texas town thirty miles east of San Antonio, and reflects the world of the pre-civil rights and pre-Vatican II era. It is an effort to share what it was like growing up as a Mexican-American in an Anglo-dominated and segregated town before the Chicano Movement. It is also the story of being a Hispanic Protestant in a Mexican-American Catholic community at a time when Catholic-Protestant relations were nonexistent. To some extent, it is the story of many Mexican-Americans in the Southwest and of Latinos in other parts of the United States, who, because of their ethnicity and religious traditions, were subjected to marginalization, separation, and pain. Yet it is also the story of the affirmation of ethnicity and religious heritage as central to ethnic self-identity. It is the exploration of my formation, ethnic and religious, and the discovery of the significance of family, church, and community.

I offer this book not just as a memoir but also with the desire to share insights into the experiences of others who are both Latino and Protestant. Latinos are the fastest-growing ethnic population in the United States; it is a diverse population with regard to national origin and also with regard to religious identity and tradition. In a larger sense, I offer this book in the hope that it will help to bring about greater understanding of Latino Protestants, Mexican-American Protestants in particular.

The examination of the formative influences of family, church, and community involves personal introspection and historical reflection. Thus this is the story of *mi familia* and my hometown as I saw and experienced them between 1943, when I was born, and 1960, when I left Seguin as a seventeen-year-old to continue my education elsewhere. It is the story of how my family and hometown shaped my early life experiences and, eventually, my self-understanding and identity.

I was reared in a Hispanic home, extended family, and barrio whose cultural and ethnic identity was Mexican-American. These sources grounded my ethnic identity as a Mexican-American. I was also nurtured in a religious family for whom the church was a center of activity. My religious upbringing was Protestant, influenced by Hispanic Protestantism and shaped by the local *iglesia metodista* (Methodist church). These realities placed me in a peculiar situation—I was a Mexican-American in an Anglo-dominated town, and I was a Protestant in a Catholic barrio. I was a member of an ethnic minority in the larger context of Seguin, and I was a member of a religious minority in my own barrio.

To be born to a Mexican-American family and to live in a Texas barrio during this historical period was to experience conditions before the social reforms of the 1960s and 1970s. Overt discrimination, segregation, and prejudice were part of daily life. Our neighborhood was poor and showed the neglect that accompanies social and political marginality. Our neighborhood west of Guadalupe Street contrasted dramatically with the rest of Seguin. Our streets went unpaved for many years, and we never had a paved sidewalk. As Latinos, we were assigned to the school for Mexican-Americans—Juan N. Seguin Elementary School. Our social world was totally separate from the Anglo world, including such institutions as barbershops, beauty shops, churches, bars, and restaurants. In addition, we were outside the sphere of political and economic influence. I do not recall a single case of a Mexican-American being elected or appointed to a public position during that era. Two Hispanic teachers at Juan N. Seguin Elementary School held the most prestigious positions among Mexican-Americans.

My Chicano neighborhood fully enjoyed its culture. The dominant language was Spanish, the sounds and smells were Mexican, our worldview was religious, and the family and social structures were grounded in the Mexican-American heritage. To grow up in such a social environment was to be formed by its cultural dynamics, to participate in the surrounding culture, and to identify with it.

To the Anglos, we were "Mexicans," or, as it was most commonly and derogatorily pronounced, "Meskins." We were defined externally, primarily according to racial categories rather than culture or ethnicity. Rare marriages between a Mexican-American and an Anglo were considered "mixed." Anglos made reference to "Mexican blood" and the "Mexican race." However, in the barrio, we also referred to ourselves as "Mejicanos," that is, *mejicano* by birth or blood. Whether we had accepted an external racial definition or developed a sense of racial definition is not clear; it was a little of both. Nonetheless, we referred to people as looking *"muy mejicano."*

But we knew that being Mejicanos meant more than merely possessing racial or physical characteristics. Likewise, we knew that it did not mean that we were from Mexico. "Mejicano" was used primarily as a cultural and ethnic definition. It involved enjoying the many ethnic and cultural pleasures that family and friends provided. It included speaking Spanish, eating *comida mejicana,* listening to *música mejicana,* and doing things that Mexicanos did and enjoyed. To be a Mexicano was to enjoy *mejicano* things. What was made clear was that as a people we were Mexicanos. Thus I grew up as a "Mejicano" and developed a Mexican-American ethnic identity.

I was born into a deeply religious family and reared in the local Protestant church, La Trinidad Iglesia Metodista. I was a fourth-generation Methodist; my great-grandfather Luis Gallardo was a Methodist lay preacher. My family on both the paternal and maternal sides had been deeply religious Protestants for generations. My grandparents were church leaders, and my parents met and courted in the church. As a child, I attended church activities several times each week and was encouraged to play a leadership role. Thus I experienced a lifestyle in which religious faith and church involvement were central to daily life. My personal self-identity was solidly religious in the Protestant tradition.

As fourth-generation Protestants, our family was distanced from the first conversions. My generation never met the first converts, nor were we told their story. We did not know what it would have been like to have been Catholic and to have converted to Protestantism. What we did know was that we were continuing a very long Protestant tradition.

However, Roman Catholicism was the dominant religious tradition in my neighborhood. I was therefore different from the rest of the residents of my barrio. But it was not simply a matter of being different and in the minority. In the pre-Vatican II era our Mexican-American community, like other communities in other parts of the world, was divided between Catholics and Protestants. The division was not simply one of religious diversity; *católicos* and *protestantes* were mutually antagonistic. I not only lived in the shadow of Our Lady of Guadalupe Church, but I also witnessed and was touched by the rivalry between religious traditions that spiritually and socially divided our community.

Who I am today is to a large extent the result of my early life in Seguin, in my neighborhood, in my church, and in my family. My initial identity was shaped by the nurturing I received from family and church. However, as I grew older and was exposed to external social realities, the ethnic and racial practices and structures of the broader community also shaped me. Like many other Latinos, my self-understanding reflects the confluence of ethnic identity and religious identity.

Although one can talk analytically about ethnicity and religious identities as two distinct types of identity, they are integrated in the self-identities of individuals, families, and communities. Self-identity integrates ethnicity and religious life, which are intimately joined in daily experiences, social interactions, personal self-understanding, and worldviews of individuals and groups who share common experiences and perspectives.

Ethnic identity and religious identity are not mutually exclusive or incompatible. To possess a Latino ethnic identity does not preclude a Protestant identity. Historically, Latino cultures and identities have deep roots in Christianity and indigenous spirituality. What is central to the Latino is spiritual life and a religious worldview. Latino Protestants are within that tradition. They hold firmly to their cultural traditions and ethnic identities while confessing a Protestant faith and spirituality. Their participation in Latino Protestant congregational life and worship further reinforces the union of their ethnic and religious realities. The existence of hundreds of Hispanic Protestant congregations speaks to the integration of Latino ethnicity and the Protestant faith in the lives of thousands of Latinos. I am a product of such a union, and I learned to be proud of and active in both my ethnic community and my religious community.

Ethnic and religious identities are important forms of diversity in the broader community as well as in the Latino communities. Most Latino identities reflect nations of origin, for example, Mexican-American, Puerto Rican, Cuban, Guatemalan. Most Latinos are mestizos, reflecting native and Spanish backgrounds;

many, especially Cubans, Puerto Ricans, and Caribbeans, are of African heritage. Latinos also are diverse in terms of religious practice: there are Roman Catholics, Pentecostals, Jews, main-line Protestants (Methodists, Presbyterians, Lutherans), Baptists, Mormons, Jehovah's Witnesses, Seventh Day Adventists, and more.

As I reach the fullness of my middle age and reflect on the many side trips and stops I have made in my life journey, I find it important to seek understanding of who I am and why. There have been many experiences that have influenced my outlook on life and the world around me. I have met many people along the way and read more books than I can remember. Many of these have influenced my thinking and action. Yet when I ask who I am and what I am about, I am driven to search much deeper. It is then that I come home. Coming home has meant exploring my initiation into life and the world and examining those social institutions that shaped my life then and have shaped who I am today.

What are the sources of my formation? Why is my family, both extended and nuclear, so important to me? Why is my identity as a Mexican-American so strongly grounded? Why do I enjoy the ethnic and cultural aspects of being a Mexican-American? Why do I cling to the Latino Protestant Church and identity? Why am I intrigued by the Catholic Church, and why do I want to learn more about it? Why is the memory of discrimination, segregation, and prejudice (both religious and ethnic) so real and powerful still? The search for answers and understanding has taken me back to where it all started. My search brings me back to Seguin, my hometown, my family, my barrio. It was here that I was born, nurtured, and where I have sought to understand myself.

These reflections took me back to Guadalupe Street. It was there that I was born and where I learned my first lessons about the world in which I was to live. Guadalupe Street taught me about barriers and divisions created and maintained through tradition, ignorance, and lack of mutual trust and openness. Guadalupe Street separated Mexican-Americans from the broader world dominated by the Anglos. It separated the haves from the have-nots. Guadalupe Street also separated my family from Our Lady of Guadalupe Church, which served our Mexican-American community. It was a deeply religious, social, and personal division. However, I learned to cross Guadalupe Street in many ways. I became bilingual and bicultural, and I learned to survive in the Anglo world. But, most of all, I have crossed Guadalupe Street to seek understanding and appreciation of the rich religious history and traditions of the Catholic Church in the Hispanic community. I have learned to be a citizen of the larger society as well as an appreciative member of the larger Hispanic family. I crossed Guadalupe Street.

A Small Town

Seguin is named after Juan Seguin, a Tejano who played an important role in the Texas War of Independence. When I lived there, it was even smaller than it is today. It seems that everyone in a small town eventually knows everything about everybody. There is no anonymity. In the Seguin that I remember, it seemed that everyone knew your name, where you lived, what you did, and who your grandfather was. *"Dime quién es tu abuelo"* (Tell me who your grandfather is), the old man asked me as he grabbed my head to get a closer look at me. "Samuel Maldonado," I answered sheepishly. My answer immediately defined me and placed me in the familial and social structures of the Mexican-American community of Seguin. It told the old man where I lived and who my grandfather and my father were and who my father had married. The old man could probably tell me many stories about both my grandfather and father.

In a small town everyone knew you or knew about you. You went to school with all the other kids in your barrio, and so you knew all about them as well. If they were not your cohorts, they were cohorts to your older or younger siblings, and so you were known as the little brother or the older brother of someone who was also known in the community—*el hermanito de Amelia,* or *el hermano mayor de Emma.* It seemed that all the adults also knew each other, because they too had gone to school together and grown up in Seguin. So you were also known as somebody's child—*el hijo de Anita Molina* or *de David Maldonado.* Who you were was known to all.

While being known to everyone in your neighborhood provided a great deal of comfort and security, it also made life a public matter. Walking down the street, playing in the neighborhood, going to church, cruising down Austin Street, or being with a girl were activities played out in a public arena. It seemed that Seguin was one big eye and one big ear. There were very few secrets, and little could be hidden. What you did became a matter of public knowledge, gossip, conversation, or debate, depending on the nature of your actions. Everyone knew when our cousin, Johnny, had been jailed again for public intoxication, or a young girl became pregnant. Whatever you did or said became public information and part of the public record. Life in a small town such as Seguin was an open book to be read and interpreted by your entire community.

Word traveled fast in a small town like Seguin. It seemed that reports or *chismes* (gossip) about your actions, words, and whereabouts were immediately known, sometimes even before you returned home, or by the time you went to school the next day, and certainly by Monday morning. Your parents were waiting for you prepared with a full report of where you had been seen and with whom. They had heard from *comadres* (godmothers), *familiares* (intimates), *vecinos* (neighbors), amigos, or the neighborhood gossip. Your schoolmates were already comparing notes by the time you walked onto the school grounds. Secrets did not last long. What you thought was private or unseen soon become public discourse.

For example, when a couple eloped, the entire town got word by the next morning or at least by Monday. It seemed that people eloped on weekends, usually from a dance. *"Se la robo del baile," or "Se fueron del baile"*—"He stole her from the dance," or "They left from the dance." Such matters were publicly discussed along with all the juicy details of who, when, and how. Young people discussed such matters as who helped and where they went. Parents would talk about the *vergüenza* (shame) for the family honor and the pain of the parents.

Because everyone knew everybody, certain events were of public concern. The sounds of ambulances and fire engines could be heard throughout town. So people would stop to listen, and many would offer a prayer. It was important to find out the direction the emergency vehicles were going. People would run out of their houses to see where the fire or the car accident was. Kids would jump on their bikes, women would run down the street, and men would jump into their trucks to get to the fire or the accident. This was done out of more than mere curiosity. It was highly probable that you knew the person involved.

Small towns like Seguin possess deep memories. Your actions, words, or accomplishments, as well as your misfortunes, could become part of the town memory, not to be forgotten anytime soon, and certainly not by your generation. Your deeds could become part of town lore, passed on to the next generations. They could become part of the town's accumulated wisdom and heritage, as a good example or as a bad example, as a precedent, or as a humorous story to be retold again and again. To this day, we talk about the escapades of "El Shorty" and Don Adolfo. We laugh at stories of El Shorty standing in the middle of the street calling out for his wife, and at gossip of Don Adolfo's behavior in the gravel pit, although these events happened more than thirty years ago and both men are long dead.

Small towns have a way of defining you. Because you are well known, it seems that your personal characteristics are also well known. Thus small towns like Seguin would give nicknames to people based on how they looked, how they spoke, where they lived, or anything that would help to describe, but also to define, the individual, sometimes for life. For example, in Seguin, "El Shorty" was a man of short stature and "El Prieto" a boy who was dark skinned. "El Güero" was a light-complexioned boy, "Speedy" walked slowly, and "La Rana" (The Frog) was a young man who lived in a neighborhood where there were many frogs. Some of these nicknames could be cruel, such as the girl who was called "La Roña" (The Rash) because she was disliked, or the girl who was called "La Bloodhound" because she supposedly looked like a dog.

There was no escape from who you were or at least how you were perceived or defined. Your public identity was determined externally by your family and its reputation, the barrio where you lived, even by personal characteristics. You were defined by things beyond your control—not that you wanted to deny certain aspects of your life. On the contrary, you might be quite proud of your family's name, its reputation, and its position in the community; you might identify closely with your barrio and be quite pleased with your natural attributes. The point is that small towns defined and described their members as a normal part of life.

However, small towns such as Seguin also defined their residents on the basis of other perceived characteristics. While those who lived in the barrio knew and defined you on the basis of personal characteristics with which they were familiar, those in the larger community defined you on the basis of impersonal characteristics, especially ethnicity or race. The larger town did not know you, yet it defined you as a "Mexican" or a "Negro." This definition was based simply on what people saw; there was limited personal contact, knowledge, or experience between racial or ethnic groups.

Nonetheless, you were defined as a "Mexican," and all the racial and social expectations of what a "Mexican" was like were attributed to you. You were known as a Mexican first, then as whatever you were or did. Thus you were a Mexican baby, Mexican kid, Mexican barber, Mexican worker, Mexican maid, or whatever else "Mexicans" did.

If there was more personal contact, you might be called "Spanish." This meant that you were more acceptable and not like the rest of the Mexicans. "Spanish folk" supposedly possessed all the positive characteristics, while Mexicans possessed all the negative ones. "Spanish" was also used so as not to insult you or whomever the discussion was about. For example, reference could be made to a "Spanish lady" but seldom to a "Mexican lady." "Spanish" was the more acceptable term and was used in formal settings. Nonetheless, my father's (Texas) birth certificate described him as "Mexican."

The town's social structure was well established and could not be changed by an individual. In a small town like Seguin, you learned your place and how to live with the social realities of the times. This does not mean that Mexican-Americans were pleased with or passive about their lot; on the contrary, there was a great deal of criticism of and sarcasm about social institutions and their "leadership." Life was a matter of survival. To go against the established powers was to ask for frustration or retaliation. You could be defined as a troublemaker, a malcontent, a person who did not know his or her place. For the sake of their jobs, their personal safety, and the welfare of their families, Mexican-Americans learned to live with many undesirable circumstances.

In essence, to be a Mexican-American was to be of lower status than Anglos, and thus less desirable, and to be avoided other than for labor. In small towns like Seguin, race and ethnicity were public definitions and determined social structures, human relations, economics, and political accessibility; they defined your place in that mini-society.

Religious tradition or identity was another important basis on which people were defined in Seguin. In the barrio, you were defined as either Protestant or Catholic. Religious identity was not simply a personal matter; it was also a public definition. You were defined as an outsider or an insider, as a heretic or a true believer, as saved or condemned, depending on which side was defining you. In small-town barrios where there was one Catholic church and one Protestant church, membership and participation in either was considered a public statement and thus determined how you were defined. Because we attended *la iglesia metodista,* we were called *protestantes,* or *aleluyas.* The former was considered derogatory; the latter, a form of teasing.

Religious and church activities such as worship, Mass, youth groups, or fiestas were also a public matter. Your attendance and participation were noticed. Religion was not a private matter; it was a public act. Thus, if you were Protestant, you could not be seen at a Catholic event; and if you were Catholic, you could not afford to be seen attending a Protestant activity. Weddings and funerals were exceptions, although many persons would wait outside the church for the religious part to be completed before joining the fiesta or funeral procession.

Life in a small town was one in which options were limited. As Mexican-Americans, there was only one elementary school we could attend. The other schools were for Anglos or African-Americans. There was one swimming pool where Mexicans were welcomed. There were two barbershops for us, and some restaurants where we knew not to seek service. Mexican-Americans were essentially limited to blue-collar jobs or manual labor. Yet some of us began to take jobs as sales clerks in downtown department stores, to graduate from Seguin High School, and to engage Anglos as friends. Nonetheless, for the majority of Mexican-Americans, life in a small town such as Seguin was one of limited options and limited public identity.

Because of the public nature of everyday life in a small town, the manner in which people are defined, and their corresponding limitations, many normal aspects of life take on added significance. The impact of such matters as personal characteristics, family membership, religious identity, and ethnicity are amplified and thus have a great impact on one's self-understanding and identity. What might go unnoticed in a large city takes on added and public significance in a small town such as Seguin. What might be considered a private matter in a larger city is a public act in a small town.

¿De Dónde Eres? / Where Are You From?

Soy de Seguin—I am from Seguin. That's what I usually say when people ask where I am from. Although I left Seguin almost forty years ago, when I was seventeen years old, and have since lived in several places, including El Paso on the U.S.-Mexican border, California, and the Dallas–Fort Worth area, I still say I am from Seguin. To say this is to acknowledge the profound influences that childhood experiences and social context have on early formation and worldview. I first experienced the world and saw it through the contextual lenses of a small town deep in the traditions of the pre-civil rights and pre-Vatican II era. As the place and time of my beginnings, it provided me with a dynamic social historical context that has served me throughout my life. Seguin was my living classroom. *Mi familia y la gente* (my family and the people) were my teachers and mentors. The church was my second home. The social structures and institutions of that small town were my introduction to the broader realities of U.S. society.

I lived in Arlington, Texas, for twenty-five years, and I now live in Denver. Yet when the question is, *¿De dónde eres?* Where are you from? "Seguin" is my response. As a college student, I lived in El Paso and found it to be an exciting border city and an excellent introduction to Mexico and the Southwest. I fell in love with the southwestern desert and the mountains of New Mexico. I worked among farmworkers in western Kansas in the 1960s during President Lyndon Johnson's War on Poverty, and I learned to appreciate agricultural life and the beauty of the farmlands. During my graduate work at the University of California at Berkeley, I lived in the San Francisco Bay Area for four years and enjoyed the climate, cultures, and natural beauty of northern California. All of these experiences have been part of my life journey and have contributed to my formation at later stages of life. But it is Seguin that provided the foundation of who I am.

Until very recently I lived in a suburb of a large metropolitan area and worked in Dallas. The large city and its suburbs had much to offer—restaurants, movies, theaters, malls, professional sports, universities, employment, and the appeal of a cosmopolitan population. I enjoyed the choices, the anonymity, and the accessibility to whatever my money could buy. I commuted thirty miles on a complex system of freeways, drove around downtown Dallas, and passed luxurious homes, barrios, and poor neighborhoods each day. I read the *Dallas Morning News* at breakfast every morning, listened to National Public Radio as I drove to work, and watched cable television in the evenings. I taught at a major university. All of these experiences and others helped to shape my daily life and how I viewed the world. Yet Seguin is still an important component of the perspective through which I interpret the world that surrounds me today. I may function in the world today as a middle-aged professional and middle-class Hispanic, but I cannot forget my beginnings as a Mexican-American boy in segregated Texas. I am active in Hispanic Protestant-Catholic dialogue and activities, yet I recall the deep gaps that separated us in Seguin. I may have left Seguin, but I will remain forever rooted there.

I find it interesting and revealing that when my wife and I mentioned that we might move into Dallas to be closer to the university and my work, both of our sons immediately reacted with astonishment. How could we even consider selling their home? I was dramatically reminded that it was our children's home and they were deeply attached to it, and they too had their own set of memories of our house and neighborhood. It was their hometown, and they made it clear to us that they wanted to be able to come back to their home and share it with their children. And so it goes.

Many of us have a special place and time that we consider home. This is not to deny the significance of marriage, home, family, and community. These are extremely important and are central elements in our daily lives as adults. I am referring to "home" as the place and time of our beginnings and early formation. Home is where we learned who we were and developed our first sense of identity. It is where it all began—where we were first influenced, shaped, and guided in a certain direction. We received our bearings and sense of the world from key persons, relationships, experiences, and events in this place and time we all call home.

Seguin is home in the sense that it represents my beginnings and formation. It is that particular place and time in which family, church, and community shaped my outlook and contributed to my self-identity. When I say "Seguin," I am not referring simply to a town defined by geography and boundaries. I have in mind a multitude of individuals who through their words, behavior, and lives taught me about very important things in life such as *sacrificio, trabajo, y educación*—sacrifice, work, and education. "Seguin" refers to a number of relationships—family, friendships, and church—that provided support, encouragement, and a set of values, many of which are still in place. These include *el respeto, familia, obligación, fe, y caridad*—respect, family, obligation, faith, and kindness. Seguin is also a number of experiences and events that provided me with insights about the world and how I was to fit in that world. The church, public schools, working downtown, and life in the barrio taught me about culture, race relations, and self-identity. Because I no longer live in Seguin and am forty years older does not mean that these influences have been forgotten or that they have faded away. On the contrary, what I learned in Seguin has been invaluable on my journey through other places and times.

Seguin and Identity

It seems that among Chicanos, identifying with a geographic place is important. I find it revealing that whenever I meet another Chicano or Latino, one of the first questions exchanged is where we are from. We tend to identify with a particular place or region—*"Soy Tejano,"* or *"Soy del valle"*—I am from Texas or I am from the Texas valley. If we are from a larger city, we tend to identify with a particular section, such as the West Side of San Antonio, South El Paso, East Los Angeles, or the Mission District in San Francisco. I guess those of us who are from small towns can claim the whole town. I am from Seguin!

In El Paso, I lived in El Segundo Barrio, the Second Ward, known as a tough and poor barrio on the south side of El Paso, immediately adjacent to the border. That was my residence. However, I was not from El Segundo Barrio. People who lived there were respected; I was an outsider and could not claim it as my own. Only those with roots in that community could claim it as their place and could assert that they were from there. Identity is far too important to be claimed so easily or to be changed from one place to another. Nor can you be from two places at once. *Eres o no eres*—either you are or you are not. There can be no confusion or misrepresentation. It is not uncommon, after claiming identification with a certain place, that you will be tested to see whether you are indeed from there and how well you know it. In many cases, it becomes a matter of having to explain that you were born in one place but reared in another, which is really where you are from.

Identification with a place can be a serious matter. It can get you into trouble, or perhaps give you favored status. You can be from the wrong side of town or from the wrong town. In Seguin it was believed that if you were from New Braunfels, you were from the wrong town. For Seguin guys to cruise New Braunfels or to date a girl from there was to ask for trouble. The same was true for guys from New Braunfels in Seguin. Your place of identity can also bring special status or relationships. Being from Seguin has since been the basis of special relationships with many persons, Anglos and Latinos, whose primary connection with me has been that we were both from Seguin. We can identify with certain locations, characters, events, and relationships that were manifested in a particular way in Seguin.

This leads to the question of how you determine where you are from. I say that I am from Seguin. What does that mean? It means several things to me. First of all, it means that I was born in Seguin on Guadalupe Street. That is where I came into this world, screamed my first *grito,* and left my umbilical cord. Seguin is where I took my first breath and was welcomed by *mi familia.* There can only be one birthplace in the life of an individual, and the relationship between that individual and that place is for life. For some, birthplace is a fleeting place lost in one's past, remembered only when filling out a bureaucratic form. However, for others, such as myself, *la tierra de mi nacimiento* (the land of my birth) holds a special place in memory and remains important for a lifetime.

One such role is a sense of mutual belonging and ownership. *Soy de Seguin* means not only that I am from Seguin but also that Seguin belongs to me in a special way. I claim Seguin in the sense that I possess experiences and memories of Seguin that are uniquely mine. This does not mean that others do not recall similar experiences in their own lives; on the contrary, my experiences are like those of many other Latinos from Seguin, as well as from Texas, other border states, and probably other regions in the United States. I experienced my hometown from within, and in so doing I developed a lifelong relationship with it. The Seguin that I remember belongs to me in a deeply personal way and is part of me.

Soy de Seguin also means "I belong to Seguin." It means that I am part of Seguin and that Seguin has a claim on me. I feel a deep sense of loyalty and belonging. I am a son of Seguin, and it has left its mark on me. No matter how far I travel, how far away I live, or how much I have changed, I am still from Seguin.

Our childhoods and hometowns have a lasting reality. Our experiences as children in our families, barrios, and hometowns remain cemented in our memories. They cannot be denied, undone, or changed. This does not mean that we are passive victims or products of an irrelevant past long gone. Nor does it mean that we do not change and evolve with the passing of time and the accumulation of experience. Life is indeed a dynamic, ever changing process of constant becoming. Nonetheless, our childhoods and hometowns make up a permanent reality that we recollect and view from the distance of many years and experiences, and in which we see and seek to understand our families, our communities, and ourselves.

Being from Seguin and identifying with it, however, does not blind me to the memories and realities of being a little Mexican-American boy in a small Texas town during the 1940s and 1950s.

Growing up in a segregated Seguin has left its painful scars that are just as unforgettable as all the pleasant experiences. To be from Seguin means to have experienced the realities of living in a poor Mexican barrio, attending Mexican schools, watching your father ride off to work on a bicycle, watching your mother take in washing, and picking cotton in the summers. It includes all the corresponding status and treatment of being Mexican in an Anglo-dominated town. To be from Seguin means having grown up in a town of divisions and boundaries. Such experiences are rooted in my memory, and they reemerge every time I return to Seguin. Nonetheless, and maybe more consciously than I care to realize, I claim Seguin and those experiences as part of who I am as well.

Being from Seguin also means experiencing the bitter and confusing Catholic-Protestant divisions in the Mexican-American community. Mutual ignorance and prejudice between Catholics and Protestants separated our families and community. We were not allowed to share, examine, or experience each other's religious traditions. On the contrary, each was warned against the other. The anti-Catholic and anti-Protestant mind-sets and behaviors left a deep mark on my memory and spirit; I am still working on it. The memory of marginality in the Hispanic community because of my Protestant faith was as painful as being marginalized by the broader community because of my ethnicity. I saw too many friendships lost and too many families split because of religious prejudice. Seguin taught me that I was Protestant and that this meant a peculiar social and religious journey. I was both a Latino and a Protestant.

To define a particular place and a particular time as significant to your identity is to recognize their lasting impact. I was reared in a Mexican-American barrio by a Mexican-American extended family. Thus, I am deeply rooted in my ethnic culture. I did not speak English until I went to public school. My family structure, home ambiance and diet, and the music I heard were all Mexican-American. Such early cultural formation has left a lifelong appreciation and love for my culture. Thus, in my case, to be from Seguin means to be Mexican-American.

Likewise, when I think of Seguin, I think of that little Mexican Protestant church that played such a key role in my early life. To be from Seguin also means to have been from that church and to have been shaped by it. It means to recall my grandmother singing hymns, Sunday school, praying at the church altar, attending vacation Bible school, singing in the choir, and wearing a suit every Sunday. To a large extent, that church is still my church and my religious identity is deeply grounded in it.

I will probably never live in Seguin again. I remember my mother telling me about the excellent college in town, Texas Lutheran College, and asking if I planned to teach there and thus return to Seguin. I remember telling her that I would probably never teach at TLC, which meant that I would not live in Seguin again. She has not asked me that question again since my father died.

802 North Guadalupe Street

The house that was home during my entire childhood until I left for college in 1960 is located at 802 North Guadalupe Street. My mother still lives there; it has been her home since July 21, 1940, when she and my father first moved in. It started out as a tiny wooden frame house composed of one bedroom and a kitchen. My father and *papagrande* (Grandfather) built this house on the lot they had bought together and divided in half. My father built his house on half of the lot, and Papagrande on the other half. The lot was much longer than it was wide, and half the lot in the back was part of a gravel pit. The house had a tin roof and wooden exterior walls painted white with green trim. The two-room house was built on cedar posts several feet above the ground, high enough for a grown man to crawl underneath.

The house grew as the family grew, and as money or materials became available. It was originally rectangular, with the kitchen and the bedroom of equal width. The first major addition to the house was a new kitchen behind the old one, which was converted into a bedroom; as a result, to enter the kitchen from the front of the house, you had to walk through the two bedrooms. There were no hallways. The addition that I remember best is the current kitchen. It seems that my parents kept adding new rooms at the back of the house; these new rooms were usually kitchens, and the old kitchens were converted into bedrooms. Making additions to the house involved the extended family—uncles, grandparents—and on occasion a skilled worker from the barrio. It was not uncommon to use scrap wood and secondhand nails. I still remember Dad's old paint cans filled with rusty, used, and bent nails that had to be straightened before they could be used on the house. The walls composed of wood of many colors and sizes were quite a sight, like a colorful puzzle.

My dad built the last kitchen—the third one he built—big enough to accommodate the large family. It was wider than the bedrooms, so it made the house L-shaped. Dad also added what became a dominant feature and the most popular part of the house (besides the kitchen), *el portal.* This porch ran along the two bedrooms and was connected to the kitchen. It had a flat roof, also made of tin.

El portal became the place where we sat on summer nights as a family and hosted the extended family or friends. The adults, especially my *abuelitos* (grandparents), would sit on green metal chairs that were not really rocking chairs but had a bounce to them; these chairs lasted so long that they had been painted several different colors in their lifetimes. When the need arose, Mother brought out the wooden chairs from the kitchen. Babies were laid on towels or blankets spread out on the floor, and covered with a light cloth to protect them from mosquitoes, flies, and other bugs of the evening.

The rest of us would sit on the *portal* floor or near the edge with our feet hanging over the side. Dad would slice a watermelon he had cooled in a basin of water all day long, or Mother would serve lemonade made from freshly squeezed lemons in a yellow-tinted pitcher. *Mamagrande* (Grandmother), cousins, and *tías* (aunts) would come over and sit on the porch enjoying the refreshments, the evening, and the *plática* (conversation). The kids would be out chasing lightning bugs or trying to find the mysterious crickets. Sometimes the evening did not bring any cooling effect, and the women would fan themselves and their babies with one hand as they tried to eat watermelon with the other. Because the porch faced the street, it was also a place from which the entire family could greet friends and neighbors as they passed by. In a real way, the *portal* served as the gathering place for the extended family, a forum where the day was reviewed and news was exchanged. In the days before television, the *portal* was our entertainment center as well. This was the place to hear family stories, greet friends, or merely enjoy a slice of cold watermelon on a hot Texas evening.

The *portal* was also our playground and, on occasion, a place to take naps when the house was too hot during the summer. Naps after lunch were a ritual in the summers whenever Mamagrande was in charge. I still think that these naps were not only for our benefit, but for her benefit as well. She needed a good nap herself after dealing with us all morning. Sometimes she would lie next to us, supposedly to ensure that we would sleep. However, she also slept, but ever so lightly so that whenever we stirred before the designated time to awaken she was ready to push our heads back down onto the pillow. *"Duerman porque esta muy caliente y si no descansan, les va a dar el polio"* (Sleep because it is very hot, and if you don't rest, you will get polio). The threat of polio brought fear to our hearts, and we would squeeze our eyes so that we would not get the dreaded disease. Mamagrande had a way of scaring us to sleep!

But mostly the *portal* was a place for play. My brother and I had our wooden rocking horse and toys scattered all over it. It was our space during the day. An adult was always nearby inside the house, but we felt that we were totally alone and could do whatever we wanted. Our imaginations ruled, and our toys carried out our fantasies. Horses could jump over the edge, we could fly like Superman, and cars could race across and crash. It was also the time when we could enjoy the metal chairs without adults and push them to the limit.

The *portal* was an important familial, social, and creative place in my formation. It was on the *portal* that I learned the value and joy of family, conversation, storytelling, sharing, and relaxation with friends. Probably because of that childhood *portal,* I have always wanted a porch or a deck. We finally built one recently. Today, whenever I sit on our deck and listen to the crickets, catch a glimpse of a lightning bug, sense the warmth of the evening, and sit on my modern metal chairs, I am taken back to the *portal* and longingly recall my family and those days in Seguin.

Playing under the house was a favorite pastime. We buried treasure, built hideouts, and claimed our own spaces there. During the blistering heat of the Texas summers, it was a cool place to be. The dirt under the house was our sandbox. The black dirt was always free of grass so that it was easy to dig into or smooth out, or simply comfortable enough to lie in thanks to its refreshing coolness. It was also a great place to hide during games of tag or *las escondidas* (hide-and-seek). It was an especially good place to hide when we were in trouble. It was too difficult for Mamagrande or our mother to crawl under to get us out, so we felt safe there. In a way, it was our own private area away from adults. At night, however, the space under the house became a mysterious and frightening place. Because no light could penetrate, it was extremely dark. At night the space under the house became the home of *el coocooy* (the bogeyman) and no place for children! We would become especially frightened if we heard noises, such as cats, coming from under the house during the night. But come morning, the place under the house became our playground and hiding place all over again.

Eventually our father screened in the *portal,* and it became a semi-interior room. It was still used for lounging around, eating meals on hot days, and hosting friends and relatives, but now it also offered more security and night use. It became a popular place for Dad to sleep on a folding army cot during the steamy Texas nights; on hot summer afternoons, it was where we continued to take our naps under the supervision of Mamagrande. The new place for family evening gathering was the backyard.

The screened-in *portal* offered us a new experience—we could watch rain and thunderstorms with a newfound sense of security. When we were kids lightning and thunder were both fearful and fascinating. Before we had the *portal,* Mother would always call us in when lightning or thunderstorms appeared, and we learned to fear them. We always associated the thunder with heaven above and thought that it meant *diosito* (God) was angry. Thus we became afraid and wondered what we had done to anger God. A favorite place to hide was under the beds. There, with pillows covering our heads and ears, we felt safe. But with the *portal,* and especially with the security of the screen, we felt that we could now look at the rain and the storms. It was a great game to see who flinched when thunder exploded above our heads.

When my sisters became teenagers, we needed bedrooms more than a playground, so Dad enclosed the walls around the portal, and it became two new bedrooms. One room was for the teenage girls, and the other was an extension of a middle bedroom where the rest of the family slept. We lost the *portal* but gained more privacy; however, because all the rooms in the house were connected, sleeping was a challenge. There were five girls, two boys, and two parents, but only two bedrooms. Needless to say, nobody had a bed to himself or herself. Instead, the two boys shared a bed, the older girls tried to fit into one double bed, and whoever was the baby slept with Mother. Dad would sleep on the cot, or wherever.

The turning off of the lights was the subject of a nightly debate. Because Dad had to get up very early to go to work, he wanted lights out early. We kids wanted to stay up to do homework. Mother was the negotiator and tried her best to help Dad get his sleep and give us a light by which to do our homework.

The last room I recall my parents adding to the house was a room built for me at the very back of the house behind the kitchen. I was a teenager and in high school. I do not recall asking for the room, nor do I recall my parents asking me if I wanted the room. They just did it. The building of this room was very special to me and made a big impression. It had two walls of windows and a large closet. It was small but large enough for a bed and even a desk. I finally had a place for my books. It was a luxury to have a private room. I could close the door and enjoy the privacy for study, sleep, or simply to lie on the bed and daydream. I was the only one in the entire family who had a private room.

What had been the entire original house was now the living room. This room, *la sala,* was not an everyday room, however. Mother had it fixed up with fancy furniture, which was covered with sheets most of the time. It was where all the formal family pictures hung on the walls. The coffee table, lamp table, and piano were covered with fancy crocheted pieces, all done by Mamagrande. We were not allowed to enter this room, much less play in it; it was out of bounds unless there was a special function. The piano was located there, so we could use the room to practice piano lessons or join in some singing. It was the place where Mother set the Christmas tree, and where we opened our Christmas presents every year. This was the room where we hosted out-of-town guests. They had to be special to get the living room treatment! Most everyday guests were received in the kitchen. The living room was also the room where my sisters hosted suitors and where Mom and Dad received and grilled these suitors.

The most popular and most frequently used room in the house was the kitchen. It was the center of family life, where we talked, entertained visitors, enjoyed meals, studied, and had *meriendas* (snacks), especially during the winter months. It served as the everyday entryway and exit of the house. The exterior kitchen door opened to the backyard and the parking area, so this is where Dad would come in after work and have his daily afternoon coffee and *pan dulce* (Mexican pastry), and where we received company and served them coffee as well.

Family meals had a pattern. We never had breakfast with Dad, because he left between 5:00 and 6:00 A.M. to go to work at the golf course. And because we had to get ready for school with only one bathroom, breakfast was a quick stop at the kitchen table where Mother had breakfast *taquitos* or Cheerios. However, dinnertime was always a family affair. We ate together as a family. It was the special event of the day. *"Vengan a comer"*—Come and eat—Mother would call out. Dad would appear washed from his waist up, and he would sit at his usual spot. He would look down at his place and wait to be served by Mother. However, dinner would not begin until everyone was sitting at the table, especially Dad. He would always sit at one corner, and Mother sat next to him. The food was served family style with the usual bowls of Spanish rice, beans, and a stack of freshly made tortillas. The main course could be a stew of hamburger meat with potatoes, chili con carne, or whatever Mother could create with half a pound of meat. The girls were always responsible for cleaning and washing the dishes.

Mealtime was a formative experience. It provided a setting where we could be a family, and we were encouraged to have conversation around the table. Table talk revolved around events of the day, school, church activities, chores, and any special issues of interest to us. Our parents were the models of a traditional Mexican-American couple who loved and respected each other. Dad came to the table in his work clothes, and Mom served the family cheerfully. We were taught to respect and listen to our parents. Likewise, we learned that feeding and caring for the family was important above all else. Our meals were not fancy; we ate what there was to eat and we were expected to be grateful. There seldom were any leftovers.

The big kitchen table served not only as the family meal table but also as the study table. Study time was always an important evening ritual. We would clear the table and spread out our books. Normally, there would be four or five kids doing homework, each at a different grade level. Before I was old enough to go to school, I used to envy my older sisters who had homework to do. I would pretend that I also had homework. Later, when I was in school, I found those study periods to be great tutoring sessions as well; there was always someone who could help with your homework. Those sessions and the encouragement we received, especially from our mother, who would do anything she could for us and get us anything we needed for school, were powerful influences on our scholastic development. We were taught that getting an education was our most important task. Nothing was to get in the way of school. Seeing our parents work hard so that we could go to school has been a source of determination and motivation for us all.

Since there was always something cooking, the kitchen was always the warmest room in the house, especially during the winter. There was always somebody in the kitchen, and this was where we hung out. Mother usually had a pot of pinto beans cooking, and its garlic aroma filled the entire house. As mealtime neared, you could smell the rice cooking in a flat skillet, and you could almost taste the tomato, comino, and cilantro as their aromas drifted through the air. When you smelled the tortillas toasting on the hot *comal,* we knew that it was almost time for dinner. It was the family room, but it was also where my mother and her cooking ruled.

We also had an outhouse, which of course served an important function. We called it *el escusado,* and we referred to going *afuera* (outside). It was built as far back on our property as possible without falling into the gravel pit, and our father relocated it as the need arose. My grandparents had their own *escusado* and we had ours. Ours was a two-seater, with one seat smaller than the other; the smaller one was for children. There was also a special seat that could be placed over either seat for the very young. The *escusado* was a private place, although it had the required ventilation through the roof and on the sides. It was the side vents that presented the greatest risk for those inside, and the greatest challenge for curious kids outside. It must have been a favorite reading room for adults, because there was always a stack of newspapers in there. Since there was no electricity in the outhouse, it was important to take care of such needs before dark; after that, an older sibling was reluctantly and unhappily drafted as an escort. The other option was to go out in the dark alone.

As small children, we took our weekly baths inside the house, in the middle of the kitchen. We did not have a water heater or a bathtub. My mother would heat water on the stove and pour the hot water into a big wash basin, into which at least two of us were dipped for our baths. On many occasions, the same water would be used for another person or set of kids. During the summer, Mother set out the bathwater to be warmed by the sun, and the younger children took their baths outside in the big wash basin. We also had a huge black cast iron kettle, a *paila,* in which Mother and Mamagrande would do the laundry. They also used it to heat the bathwater when baths were taken outside.

Another outdoor activity was *la lavada*—doing the laundry. During my earlier years, there was no indoor washing machine or dryer. Dad built a shed in the backyard that served as a washroom, storage place, playhouse, and whatever. When I was a small child, I remember, my grandmother and mother did all their laundry on a washboard. They used water heated in the *paila* (iron kettle); they scrubbed the clothes by hand on the washboard, wrung the water out by hand, and hung the clothes out to dry. When there were not enough clotheslines, they used rosebushes or other bushes. Eventually, our father bought an electric washing machine that included a roller through which the clothes were wrung and readied to hang. On some occasions, however, fingers, hands, and arms would be caught in the rollers and a minor emergency would ensue.

But the clothes still had to be hung outside to dry. A popular game we played was running through the sheets and other large items hanging on the line. Getting caught in the drying laundry was practically a major offense and punishable by being made to go inside and take a nap. However, when sudden thunderstorms blew in, it was an entire family effort to rescue the laundry from the rain and bring it inside before it got soaked. This was probably the most fun for the kids.

Most of our everyday clothes were washed and dried outside. Our underwear, T-shirts, and jeans and the sheets were all dried outdoors. They had a slight stiffness and wrinkle and smelled like whatever was in the air at the time. The other clothing, especially the girls' dresses and Sunday clothes, were ironed by hand. *Dias de plancha* (ironing days) involved warming the irons, preparing the *almidón* (starch), sprinkling and rolling the pieces into small damp balls, and rhythmically ironing each piece. On those *dias de plancha,* the entire house smelled of freshly starched and slightly singed clothes. The ironed clothes were hung in the corners of the living room on special lines or on the interior doors, and, when there was no more room, they were spread out on the beds.

It was a major event when the city put in a sewer system on Guadalupe Street and we were able to have indoor plumbing. We were both shocked and excited that we could have an indoor *escusado.* We carefully watched every step of the process from the digging of the sewer line to the first flush of the commode. In addition to the commode, this meant an indoor bathtub, a kitchen sink, and hot water. No more heating water outside. No more outdoor baths. And especially, no more *escusado.* It was a marvel! What would they think of next? We felt we were so modern and so uptown.

Getting indoor plumbing ranks with the time we bought our first refrigerator. For years, we had an icebox, which literally meant a box in which ice was placed for keeping our food cool. It contained no freezer, so keeping anything frozen was out of the question. The ice melted in a matter of hours, and taking out the melted ice was a chore performed each summer day. Every day the iceman came by, selling his blocks of ice from the top of his truck. We would run out to see him as, wearing a leather apron, he used his metal tongs to carry the ice into the house. By the following day, the ice had melted, and the process started all over again.

A popular summer event for us was when Dad purchased an extra block of ice on Saturdays and made *raspa* (snowcones) using his own hand scraper. We all gathered around him as he placed the block of ice on a table in the backyard, and we fought to be first. Our favorite flavor was strawberry, but when there was only one flavor available, you took what you were given. There was nothing more enjoyable and refreshing than a melting snowcone in a wet paper cone on a hot summer afternoon. Sipping the melting ice through the bottom was heaven, and sucking the stained and wet leftover paper cone offered a lingering sense of satisfaction.

Another memorable event was when we got a telephone of our very own. We did not have a telephone for many years, and most of our family had never used one before. Our means of communicating was to send an oral message with one of the more reliable older children, who would run across town or wherever the message needed to go. When the plain black telephone was installed, we could hardly wait to call someone. We had to call the operator, who would respond with "Number please." Our number was 1854J. We would tell her the number we wanted to call, and she would ring it for us. It was such a marvel to hear a voice coming out of the black box; we called our relatives just to hear their voices. Years later another breakthrough in technology in our home was the installation of a telephone with a rotary dial. We could now dial the telephone numbers ourselves, and we had great fun listening to the clicking of the rotary as it spun back into place.

Four large trees in our backyard were another important part of our childhood days on Guadalupe Street that I remember fondly. We called these trees *los palos blancos* (the white trees), or we simply referred to the area as *bajo de los palos* (under the trees). These were four alamo trees planted in a perfect square. For us kids, the trees served as a jungle gym; we would climb them as far as we possibly could, and we also built several treehouses in them. We called the treehouses our "hideouts." Once we put up an old gas pipe connecting two trees, and this became a chinning bar that we played on until our hands blistered. It also held up a swing made from an old tire. We spent many summer afternoons and evenings under the trees playing and using our imaginations until Mom called us back to reality and inside for the night.

The *palos blancos* became our father's favorite outdoor sitting place after we no longer used it for our play. He put the two metal rocking chairs back there and sat for hours on summer evenings. As young teenagers, under the shade of the trees, we listened to the radio stations from San Antonio, sang Elvis Presley songs, discussed important topics such as girls, and shared dreams of leaving Seguin someday to join the navy. On warm nights it was not uncommon for Dad to sleep under the trees on the old army cot.

Our home at 802 North Guadalupe Street was a great place to experience childhood. By today's standards, it would be classified as "low-income housing." It was a house that reflected the economic status of our parents. Certainly, it did not compare to the houses across Guadalupe Street, but it was much in line with the other houses in the barrio. We never had air-conditioning or central heating, but it was our house, and we thought it was the best one on Guadalupe Street. Each new addition was an improvement and was viewed as an affirmation of our place. It was all we knew, and we were proud of it. It was La Casa de los Maldonados.

Our home was a place where we shared daily life with siblings, extended family, and people from the barrio. Its openness reflected the attitude and lifestyle of our family. Everybody was welcomed in our home, on the *portal,* or in the backyard. But our home was also a private place where we found refuge, nurturing, and guidance. It was where we played, did our homework, and practiced the piano. It is the house that our father built for us and that our mother made into a home. Every corner of this house has a special memory of some event in the family. It was our world.

My mother still lives at 802 North Guadalupe Street, and we return to visit often. To return there is to revisit my childhood and the place where I thoroughly enjoyed my formative years. But now when I return home, I notice that the floors are uneven, and the roof leaks. The plumbing is no longer efficient. My parents closed up the crawl space underneath the house, and the four trees are gone. To return and see the aging place is sad in some respects. But it also reminds me of where I began my life, and it holds many fond memories; I am grateful for that time and place that have left their mark on me.

La Calle Guadalupe

I recall Guadalupe Street as a hodgepodge of residences, churches, and assorted community businesses. The street was lined primarily by residences, but there were also several bars, two black churches, a Catholic school, my uncle Porfirio's upholstery shop, a grain elevator, a feed store, a black funeral home, and Elmo's Grocery Store, where we bought most of our groceries. There were also three *tienditas* (little stores) on North Guadalupe Street. On the south end was Leo's *tiendita,* and on the north end was Castilla's store; at the end of our block was *la tiendita de Don Aguilar.*

Guadalupe Street was a major street running north and south on the west side of Seguin. It was an important route between the barrio and downtown and a major link between north and south Seguin. The sounds of traffic—cars honking, trucks roaring—and people walking to town or church were constantly heard in the background. We saw men on their way to work on foot, on bicycles, or in their cars. Our street was a major route to school, and so it was a great place for watching people, meeting friends, and observing the cycle of daily life in Seguin as the town passed before our eyes.

For the longest time, Guadalupe Street was a dirt and gravel road, marked by two sets of ruts created by the constant traffic. Dusting the furniture in the house was a daily chore performed by Mother and my sisters, and wetting down the yard and the street in front of our house was my grandmother's daily task. As she tried to reduce the dust that came into the house. she would say, *"Ese maldito polvo"* (This cursed dust). We did not have much of a lawn, and so the dirt yard was a daily challenge for her.

You can imagine the excitement we felt when we heard that La Calle Guadalupe was going to be paved. It changed our playing routine for several months, as watching the trucks and workers became the center of attention. We took daily note of the progress and came to know the workers and the jobs they performed. I especially remember *el mochito*—the driver of heavy equipment who had a stub for one arm but handled huge tractors with ease. We considered ourselves very fortunate to live on a paved street, and it soon became a status symbol in the barrio to live on Guadalupe Street.

The feeling of good fortune soon came to an abrupt end; when Guadalupe Street was paved it became a major thoroughfare connecting the barrio and downtown. Guadalupe Street was now a drag strip for local teenagers. And the fact that there were some bars down the street made matters worse. Cars zoomed by and people walked by at all hours of the day and night. Since the street was only about ten feet from the front of our house, it became difficult to take naps in the front rooms, so we had to go to the back. Our front yard now became a no man's land and out of bounds for our play, especially for riding bicycles. We saw more car accidents on our corner than we care to remember. The one thing we did salvage was a game that involved sitting in front of the house and claiming the next car that would come by. "The next car is mine."

Guadalupe Street also served as the great divide between the Mexican-American barrio and an old Anglo neighborhood. We lived west of La Calle Guadalupe, and the Anglos lived east of the street. We could look across the street and see the Anglo families. We followed their activities on a daily basis, but they were a world away from us and we from them. They could also see us, but I do not ever remember our families visiting each other. Once in a while there would be a wave, but that was it.

We did not cross Guadalupe Street until we went to Mary B. Erskine Junior High School. And even then, crossing Guadalupe Street was a dangerous thing to do because of the traffic. Nonetheless, I had to cross it to enter a new world—an integrated junior high school and the Anglo world—and I had to cross it again to return to my home and our Mexican-American world. In a sense, it was an ethnic and cultural boundary, separating the Mexican reality from the Anglo reality, the Spanish-speaking world from the English-speaking world. To cross Guadalupe Street was to enter an Anglo-dominated world and to learn to live in a culturally different world. Crossing back and forth meant making daily cultural transitions and adjustments between the Anglo- and the Mexican-American realities.

Guadalupe Street was also a social and economic separator. We lived on the poor side of Guadalupe Street. The Anglo side had landscaped lawns, paved streets, sidewalks, and driveways. The barrio had gravel streets, no curbs, no sidewalks, dusty yards, and houses reflecting their poor inhabitants. Crossing Guadalupe Street meant observing the striking differences between the haves and the have-nots in Seguin on a daily basis. Where you lived defined your economic status and also contributed to the gradual realization that you were from the poor part of town.

Guadalupe Street also provided a dramatic picture of the political structure of Seguin. During this era, people had to pay a poll tax for the privilege of voting. Paying for the right to vote discouraged many poor Mexican-Americans from participating in elections. As a result, Mexican-Americans were left out of the democratic process and our neighborhood was not provided with public services at the level that other parts of town received them. This was seen in the nonexistence of paved streets, sidewalks, or curbs. No elected public official lived in our barrio. No Mexican-American was ever elected to public office while I lived in Seguin.

When Our Lady of Guadalupe Church moved to La Calle Guadalupe, the street became the symbol of yet another division. It became a visual barrier between the Catholic and the Protestant realities for our family. Our Lady of Guadalupe relocated from its old site next to Mamadita's (Great-grandmother's) house to kitty-corner to our house. Guadalupe Street divided us from the church I have never entered. The Catholic church was now on Guadalupe Street, and for me the street again represented separation between two worlds—Catholic and Protestant. With the church across the street, Guadalupe Street became a daily reminder that "they" were Catholic and "we" were Protestant.

The bells from the Catholic church across the street awakened us every morning as they called people to Mass, and we watched the people from the barrio streaming to Mass every day, but we never crossed the street to attend. From across Guadalupe Street we could see our neighbors, schoolmates, and even our mother's cousins on their way to the Catholic church. As they walked to Mass, they saw us and were reminded that we were not going to Mass because we were *protestantes*. From across the street, we prepared to go to our Protestant church. Sundays were especially significant and symbolic days. On Sundays Mexican-Americans were divided according to religious tradition. We went our separate ways as we passed our Catholic neighbors and their church on our way to our Protestant church across town.

With the Catholic church across the street, La Calle Guadalupe became a major boulevard for Latino activity. An annual event on

Guadalupe Street was *la jamaica* festival and bingo. It was a big fiesta that lasted a full weekend and ran long into the night. This meant crowds of people walking, driving, and parking up and down Guadalupe Street. My dad would bring out his metal rocking chairs and some folding lawn chairs, sit in the front yard, and visit with his friends as they made their way to the *jamaica*. We watched many *jamaicas* and bingo games, heard the sounds and laughter of the crowds, and the calling of the bingo letters and numbers—"B 24," "G 45," and so on. We could smell the aromas of the fiestas—popcorn, tacos, *barbacoa* (barbecue)—and hear the clinking of bottles. We could also hear the beat of polka music and the sounds of darts popping balloons. The sounds and smells were powerful and stimulating; we could imagine being there with our friends and neighbors, but we never once made it across the street to participate. Our relatives, especially our *abuelita,* made it clear that *jamaicas* were Catholic and that, as good Methodists, we were not to attend such things. Our grandmother's pietistic understanding of what it meant to be a Christian did not allow us to engage in frivolous activities. Thus we could only watch from across the street.

The first television set on Guadalupe Street was bought by our parents and was at our house. This was an exciting event for the whole family and for the entire neighborhood. I recall that when the TV was installed all of us kids sat in front of it, watching the screen waiting for programming to start in the afternoons. We did not mind watching a silent picture with a big number in the middle as we waited for thirty minutes. This gave us an opportunity to compete for the best spot and speculate on what we would see. The entire room would soon fill with cousins, friends, and neighbors.

Wednesday nights were big nights for my father and neighbors; these were nights when boxing matches were on TV. On Saturday nights, there was wrestling. My dad would place the TV in the front window facing outside so that we could all watch it from the front yard. Needless to say, the front yard got full very quickly as people walking by would stop to watch the fights or whatever was on that night. Mother would bring out a pitcher of iced Kool-Aid, and Dad was king for the night surrounded by friends as they watched and rooted for their favorite boxer or wrestler.

Guadalupe Street was my world; it was the street on which I was born. It defined my world and shaped my early formation as a Mexican-American and as a Protestant. It set boundaries in my childhood and defined who I was. I saw it change from a dusty unpaved street to a major thoroughfare, and I knew it from birth until I left for college. La Calle Guadalupe was my street. I walked it. I learned to ride my bike on it, and eventually I learned to drive a car on it. It was my street, but it also presented me with many challenges. I am pleased to say that those early divisions—ethnic and religious—that La Calle Guadalupe represented became challenges later in life, and I have crossed it many times in my mind and relived it numerous times in my life ever since.

Mi Familia

Many would say that we were a large family—five girls and two boys. However, we thought we were an average-size family, and seven sounded like a good number to us, although we would have been eight if one of our sisters had not died at birth. I was the fourth child, which placed me right smack in the middle of my brother and sisters. There were three girls older than I am—Anita, Amelia, and Alicia; my three younger siblings were Raquel, Alejandro, and Emma. Being in the middle had its advantages and its disadvantages. I was never old enough to be responsible—there were always my older sisters around for that—yet I was never young enough to claim innocence. I was stuck in the middle!

I was also the firstborn son, which brought its own set of

privileges and pressures. Among Latinos, it is important to have a male child so that the family name will continue into the next generation. My birth meant that there would be another generation of Maldonados. I was referred to not only as *"un hijo"* (a son) but also as *"un hombrecito"* (little man). I still recall being called *"papacito"* at times, a not-too-subtle message. I cannot but think that subtly I was taught that it was important that I was a male but also that I would continue the family name and that this was desirable and expected, or at least hoped for.

During most of my years in Seguin, I had a nickname within my family and extended family. Among the Maldonados I was known as "Junior." This is simply because I was named after my father. However, my extended family on the maternal side had a difficult time pronouncing the name "Junior," especially Mamagrande and my *tías*. The problem was with the *J* and with the *-ior*. The *J*, which is difficult for a Spanish speaker to pronounce in English, was given the softer pronunciation *Y* and *-ior* was totally dropped. The outcome was "Yoon" or "Yune." Complicating the matter was that there were three cousins named Junior on that side of the family, and so it was necessary to distinguish among the three of us. This was very important, because the basic form of communication was yelling out the name of the kid being summoned. There was "Yoon Grande" (the older one), "Yoon" (the middle one), and "Yoon Chiquito" (the youngest one). I was the middle one, and so I was called simply "Yoon."

My sister Anita was the firstborn in our family and the trailblazer for the rest of us. She was the one who took the brunt of introducing our parents to parenthood. Anita had an independent mind. She was a dreamer and a risk taker, and she was quite assertive about it, too. She was a determined (some would say hardheaded) kid who did not tolerate others' opinions on matters that were important to her. She always spoke her mind and expressed her opinion, even when it differed from my parents'. As you can imagine, this resulted in being disciplined more than a few times by our parents. As younger siblings, we all watched and learned from her example. Anita was among the first Hispanics to graduate from Seguin High School; she was certainly the first from within our extended family. She was the Queen of the *Diez y Seis de Septiembre* festivities and always had a flair for fashion, cooking, and home decorating. It was she who introduced our family to new foods and drinks that she had learned in home economics class in school. I still remember the heat she took from our father when she prepared some fancy new dish, especially when it was not Mexican food. Anita was also the one who pioneered music for the family. She played the piano and loved to sing, especially Mexican music. She also played the cornet in the high school band. I have always admired her determination, drive, and willingness to work hard for whatever she set out to accomplish.

One of the events I remember that involved Anita was her high school graduation party. This was a pretty big event. She was the first Maldonado or Molina to graduate from high school, and we were all so proud. I must have been about eleven or twelve years old when this happened, not old enough to attend a high school party but old enough to observe from the fringes. Since it was held at our house, I had a good vantage point from which to watch. With her flair for decorating and preparing fancy foods and her eye for fashion, Anita was at her best for this event. Needless to say, Dad was not excited about it, but it was Anita's graduation and it was going to be held anyway. Dad managed to rent tables and benches from the city for what was probably the biggest party on Guadalupe Street that year. Mother was supportive and certainly proud. The house and yard were decorated with ribbons, and chairs were set out for the guests, mostly Anita's friends. The impressive thing for us was the food, stuff we had never seen before. As the younger ones and not really guests in the party, we had to sneak in and grab whatever we could. Anita served the fanciest sandwiches we had ever seen—chicken and tuna salad sandwiches! She had even trimmed off the crust of the triangular pieces of white bread. We had never seen this before. *And* she served fruit punch. That party really convinced us that Anita had class.

Amelia, the second child, was the quiet sister of the family. As a small child, she would cover her face with her skirt when company came to visit. Her shy ways and serious nature might have been the result of watching Anita being disciplined by our parents, or it may just have been her way of being. Amelia was the dedicated and accomplished musician of the family. She developed her piano and voice talents early and blossomed in the church as the pianist, choir director, and organist. It seems that our mother felt that if the church was going to have its own pianists, we ought to train them. Amelia stepped forward and committed herself to religious music and was successful in it throughout her life.

As kids, we called Amelia "Mele." She was named after Amelia Earhart because our mother wanted her to be as brave as the famous aviator. Mele was born on Jones Street and was delivered by Mamadita, who was a midwife. Amelia was always a thin girl, and our parents worried about her health. I still remember Mother making Mele *ponche*—a drink made of milk, raw eggs, and nutrients believed to help fatten and strengthen her. But Mele never gained weight in her youth. This was probably one reason that she chose to focus on the piano and not on a band instrument that she would have to carry while marching.

As one of the older sisters, Mele played a key role in taking care of the rest of us while Mother was at work. Amelia was a meticulous housekeeper, and I recall on many occasions being run out of the house by her and not being allowed to come back in because she had just cleaned the house. Mele, like Anita before her and the rest of us after, worked downtown. She had a job at Duke and Ayers, a dime store where she often was in charge of selling candy. I used to go in and have her wait on me. I would order a dime's worth of chocolate-covered peanuts; she would give me a bagful and return ten cents in change. Needless to say, she was my favorite dime store clerk in Seguin.

Alicia, whom we called "Licha," was the first Maldonado born at our house at 802 North Guadalupe. In many ways, she is probably the sister who is closest to me. She was the sibling immediately preceding me. I spent the most time with her at home and at school. She was a fun kid, loud and happy-go-lucky. She also had a streak of assertiveness and had an adventuresome spirit. Licha was my mentor at Juan N. Seguin Elementary School and later in junior and senior high school. She knew all the teachers and helped me with my homework. She also introduced me to band and tennis. We spent many afternoons playing our cornets together, riding bikes, and generally getting into trouble.

I remember one day when we rode our bikes all the way to the elementary school; this was farther than we were allowed to ride. Close to the school there was a steep hill, perfect for racing. So we did. Unfortunately, I lost control of my bike on the gravel and fell; Licha, who was right behind me and did not have full control of her bike, rode straight over me. She thought she had killed me. But I survived. And I learned to stay out of her way.

Raquel, or "Laque" as we called her, was also born at home on Guadalupe Street. She is two years younger than I am. Laque was *la güera* (the light-skinned one) of the family, and as a small kid some relatives called her *"la alemana vieja"* (the old German woman) because of her fair skin. We would all laugh at her because she would say *"Ero yo Laque"* (It is me, Laque). She was always a happy kid.

She started out playing the drums in the band but quickly gave that up. It was not for her, and she was not going to do something just because the rest of us had done it. Like Anita, she was independent and assertive. She, too, worked downtown at the dime store. Raquel was probably the most academically gifted of my sisters and made the honor roll in school several times. She was popular among her peers and always had lots of admirers. As her older brother, I always wondered how many boys were friendly to me because of Laque.

My brother Alejandro, whom we called "Cando," was born at 802 North Guadalupe Street. He is named after our mother's brother who died in infancy. Cando is four years younger than I am. He was carefree and fun-loving and seemed to truly enjoy being a kid. He used to follow me around and joined whatever games I was playing with cousins my age, even when he was not invited. That Cando was four years younger did not stop him from participating in our play. He joined us in *las escondidas,* cowboys and Indians, hideouts, jungle, marbles, and later, baseball. We had the usual brotherly fights over toys, and we engaged in wrestling matches from time to time. Cando did not let his age stop him, however, and he was willing to take me on any time. In fact, he was a tough little kid who grew up to be bigger than me.

Cando hated school. But he played football in junior high, and for some reason came home to shower after football practice every day instead of showering at school. He must have been a shy young man. But football was not enough to keep him in school, so he left junior high to get a job. Our father did not let Cando simply drop out of school and insisted that he get some type of training. Cando chose barber school and became a barber at the Job Corps center in San Marcos and later in the navy. He was a popular kid and made friends easily. Our house was a favorite place for them to gather.

Emma is the youngest sibling of the family. She was *la bebita* (the little baby). She was everybody's baby, and we all took care of her. We all claimed that she was the spoiled one, *la consentida,* and that she got away with things that the rest of us were never able to get away with. She hated housework and would cry her eyes out rather than wash dishes. There were always older sisters who were the caregivers and housekeepers, so Emma was frequently able to avoid both activities. She also did not care much for school, although she had the ability to do well academically. What she did do was play and dream. Of all the siblings, Emma probably had the keenest sense of humor. Needless to say, we all enjoyed her humor and gave her a hard time for avoiding the broom and dishes.

Like many poor working families who lack the proper medical attention, our parents lost a child who would have been between Anita and Amelia. She died at birth, a victim of strangulation by the umbilical cord. She is remembered as a beautiful little girl. My father built the coffin in which she was buried the same day she was born.

Being part of a large family was as much fun as it was challenging. There were always enough kids to play with, and there was never a boring moment, other than when Mamagrande forced us to take naps. We pretended that wood and rocks were our trains and cars. We played in the dirt, in the mud, under the house, in the shade of the trees, on top of the car, and in the big gravel pit behind the house. We played tag, chased after fireflies, organized baseball games, and enjoyed tennis.

The older sisters played important roles as our caregivers. Our mother worked six days a week outside the home, so we took care of ourselves, or more precisely, the older sisters were in charge. This resulted in some problems. They were often more strict than our mother. When the girls were cleaning the house, the younger kids were banned until they decided we could come back in. If we did sneak in, sat on a made bed, or tracked in dirt, we were in really deep trouble. On many occasions, our sisters carried out their form of discipline, mainly screaming and running after us as we ran through the house and out the door.

Since we were a large family, our parents had to be creative in providing food and clothing for us. My mother made many dresses for the girls that were later passed on to the younger ones. As the eldest son, I did not have to inherit any clothes from an older brother, but Cando did. I remember my mother making shirts for me; she was also a frequent user of the Sears catalog and the layaway service at local stores. Layaways were both exciting and frustrating. As an annual ritual, my mother took us to the store in early to middle summer and set aside our school clothing for the fall. It was exciting to see the new school clothes but frustrating because we could not take them home until she had finished the weekly payments. The same was true for Christmas clothes.

Shoes were a problem; our feet seemed to grow daily. We had two pairs of shoes: one pair for school and the other for church. During the summer, we ran around barefoot up to the age of twelve or so. Every day after school we were expected to take off our shoes and wear old ones or none at all. I remember my father coming home and finding us playing baseball in our school shoes and making us take them off immediately. By the end of the school year, our shoes had lost their shape, front soles, heels, and backs.

Feeding the family was also a challenge calling for creative measures. Mother stretched what we had and made do without what we did not have. Our daily staples were beans, rice, potatoes, and flour tortillas. Mother would make the tortillas daily, and she always had a pot of beans cooking on the stove. On many occasions we were sent to the neighborhood store to buy some hamburger meat; she would feed the whole family with a half pound of meat. She would make *guisos* (dishes) with chopped potatoes and hamburger meat. Kool-Aid was a favorite drink of the family but one that stressed the family budget because it required so much sugar. Mother would give Dad special attention on some occasions. She prepared special meals for him such as brains, *tripas,* and other specialties we did not recognize or care to eat! A breakthrough or change in our eating habits occurred when Anita would bring home new recipes or ideas from her home economics class. We tried meatloaf, tunafish, turkey, salads, and fancy desserts—all foods new to our palates. Anita introduced us to white bread, sandwiches, Jell-O, pudding, and other "exotic" foods from across La Calle Guadalupe.

All our meals were family style, and it was important that we all be together at mealtime. The table would be set with large bowls of beans, rice, potatoes, chile in a *molcajete* (stone grinder), and a stack of warm tortillas covered with a cloth. We were all expected to sit at our places; Mother would serve Dad and the younger ones, and then the rest of us would serve ourselves. We were expected to eat all our food and clear the table when we were finished. As I look back, our meals were special times. We came together as a family with both parents and all the children present. These were special moments, and they still nourish me.

My household played a special role in my development. It was a sanctuary from the world and a place where I was accepted, loved, disciplined, and instructed. It was part of my private world where my family shared dreams, fears, frustrations, and hope. We depended on one another, for we knew one another's needs, strengths, and weaknesses. My sisters took care of us, they mentored me through school, and they were my partners in play and study. We pushed each other and we supported each other. We taught each other and learned from each other. We had our own world of play and imagination. We shared the realities of La Calle Guadalupe and of being Protestant. We shared laughs, we cried together, and we were *nuestra familia* (our family).

With the exception of the infant who died at birth, we all lived into adulthood. Anita has had a successful career as a notary public at the Bexar County Courthouse in downtown San Antonio; she is the loving mother of two sons, Billy and Bobby, and the grandmother of two little girls and a boy. Although she lives in San Antonio, Anita and her husband, Frank, own a country home in South Texas. We kid her that our parents worked hard to escape life *en el rancho*, and she chose life in the country.

Amelia also had a successful career in public service. She worked for many years with the Texas Department of Rehabilitation, retired in Seguin, and is the only Maldonado sibling to make Seguin her permanent home. She and her husband, Danny, were active members of the church, where she played the organ regularly until her recent death. Mele was the last of the Maldonado family to be a member of La Trinidad Iglesia Metodista. She was the first of the siblings to die. Her death brought the family and almost all of Seguin together to celebrate her life and bury her in Seguin.

Alicia went to college after raising her three children and became a schoolteacher. She married José, a Methodist minister, and traveled the country and the world during his career as a U.S. Navy chaplain. Their three children, Ricardo, Cindy, and José, produced five grandchildren. Their son, José, and grandson, LJ, have been Mother's house companions during her later years.

Raquel also went to college, became a schoolteacher, and

married Ruben, a Methodist minister. They lived in Tennessee and in various parts of Texas and now reside in El Paso. Raquel and Ruben have two children, Ruben and Judy, and two grandchildren, both boys.

Cando married Irene, a young woman from Mexico, and made a career in the U.S. Army and Navy. He served as a barber and as a cook while in the military. Today he owns his own barbershop in Louisiana, and his wife owns and runs a Mexican restaurant. Cando and his wife have two children, Donna and Alma, and four grandchildren.

Emma went to college after raising her daughter and is now a teacher in New Braunfels, where she lives with her husband, Noel. Their daughter, Nancy, also lives in New Braunfels.

Dad died in June 1984 in Seguin. Mother still drives her car around Seguin, usually to church and sometimes to San Antonio. She sang in the church choir for many years and continues to participate as an active member of her Sunday school class and the church women's group. She visits her children and continues to host Christmas Eve family gatherings in Seguin. The highlight of her year is the annual family reunion.

The Extended Family

Among the pleasures of growing up in Seguin was having an extended family there. I was reared and surrounded by *abuelitos, abuelitas, tíos, tías, primos,* and *primas*, including many relatives several times removed yet known to us as *familiares* or *primos*. I was born in my grandparents' house, which was next door to the family home where I spent the first seventeen years of my life; Mamagrande was right there next door to us and intimately involved in our daily lives. Tío Beto and his family lived behind Mamagrande's house for a few years. Across the gravel pit from us lived Tía Chavela and Tío Gere and the cousins with whom I spent my childhood years. Several blocks away from us lived Mamadita, my great-grandmother; her home was a regular stopping place for us after school. Several blocks away was the Gallardo clan, a part of the Molina extended family (my mother's family). Tío Porfirio, my father's cousin, lived two houses down on Guadalupe Street and was also a daily presence in our lives. The Maldonado grandparents lived across town from us, and we visited with them weekly.

Not a day went by that I was not cared for by an *abuela* or *tía,* or that I did not play with a cousin or visit a grandparent or otherwise have some interaction with my extended family. The extended family network was thick, well populated, and very effective in embracing our daily lives. It included at least four generations and several households. Life in such a setting had its blessings as well as its challenges. An extended family composed of distinct households, living in such close proximity, and populated by a large number of children cannot avoid challenges to peace and harmony, and we had our share. It seemed that most problems had to do with the everyday lives of children living and playing together, running back and forth between houses, and sharing a common space and time, not to mention toys, hideouts, trees, and valuable artifacts of childhood. When one would get into trouble with a cousin, it was always the fault of the other household. Younger kids suffered at the hands of the older ones and many times ended up running home in tears. Toys got lost and were found in other houses. In spite of the children, the adults seemed to get along or found ways to keep their distance when the need arose.

Living in an extended family also meant an ongoing round of activities and continuous play for the younger ones. Something was always happening among us, between us, or within a particular household. This included births, birthdays, illnesses, and gossip. There was always someone or a group to play with. Play was a continuous activity that involved going from one house to another, moving from one game to another, with cousins constantly joining in and dropping out. While some of us played house or marbles in twos or threes, the rest might be playing baseball, cowboys, jungle, hideout, or tag. Our turf included several homes, yards, and an entire gravel pit. Play was interrupted by meals, when we all had to go to our respective homes, but it resumed immediately thereafter and continued until dark. And so there was always something to report at the end of the day.

The cousins with whom we spent most of our childhood were the Lunas, who lived across the gravel pit from us. Tía Chavela is my mother's only sister, and we have always known the Lunas as Tío Gere and Tía Chavela. They had a wonderful sense of humor and loved to laugh. They saw life with optimistic eyes. They both loved music, and I remember Tío Gere playing his guitar. My dad would say that he spent more time tuning his guitar than actually playing it. I think Tío Gere was shy and did not like performing in front of people.

The Luna cousins of my generation included Jerry, who we called Gerito; Agustín, who we knew as "Tin"; Christina, whose nickname was Tina; and Elia. Mando was the youngest at that time; however, the Luna family kept growing after I left home. But I have known them all as they grew up. Gerito, Tin, and I started school together, played together nonstop as children, and shared significant milestones together as we grew up in the same extended family, barrio, school, and church. We were as close as any cousins could be. Gerito was an impressive and serious kid. He was always way ahead of the rest of us in imagination and childhood experimentation. He was great at building hideouts with sticks and branches; he could make bows and arrows that he would actually use to hunt doves at Mamadita's house. As a teenager, Gerito was both musically and artistically talented. He could sing like a pro and had an Elvis hairdo with a big pompadour and long sideburns. His paintings won awards in school, and he was accomplished at playing the cornet in the high school band. In addition, Gerito was handsome and dressed with flair. I think Jerry (we called him Jerry when we became teenagers) was probably the first kid in the barrio to wear white suede shoes, black pants, and shiny shirts. Tin, his quiet, shy, little brother, inherited a great sense of humor from his parents, but he could never finish a joke because he would start laughing before delivering the punch line. Tin had a great "ear" and could play the guitar better than Jerry. As teenagers, Tin and I spent many afternoons in the backyard listening to the radio and talking about girls and about joining the navy.

As I revisit my childhood days, I realize that being a member of an extended family was important, and I miss it today. It grounded me in family and provided me with the warm comfort and security of many arms, the joy of cousins and playmates, and the freedom of knowing that there was always someone looking after me, and it helped to define me as a member of the broader family.

Memories of my extended family also include the adults. They were important actors for us children, and they shaped the ambiance and spirit for the rest of us. Their examples, words, and actions guided us as we grew. Watching the men rise before dawn to go to work and having the loving care of the women and older sisters were strong forces in shaping my sense of responsibility and caring. Participating in family gatherings in the backyard as we shared food or a watermelon and listening to the adults tell stories about their childhoods or talk about their work taught me much about sharing. Watching them cooperate in building and repairing one another's houses was a powerful lesson in mutual support. My grandparents, aunts, and uncles were an important part of my Seguin experience and formation and provided a solid foundation of love, care, and belonging.

Mamadita: The Grand Matriarch

I don't know why people insist on characterizing Latino culture, especially Mexican-American, as male dominated; my family experience has been one in which the women played the prominent, if not dominant, roles, especially on my maternal side. Beginning with my great-grandmother, women have been the center of our home and family as well as the force that shaped who we were. Whenever we referred to our great-grandmother's or grandparents' homes, it was always in terms of the maternal side—Mamadita's house, Mamagrande's house, or Mamá Emma's house. The women shaped the daily lives of their families and defined the character of their homes and families.

Amada Gonzalez (Gallardo) was my great-grandmother. She

was born on February 12, 1868, in Bexar County, Texas. Although she married Luis Gallardo, she never took his surname. Even today, as the old ones remember Mamadita, they all point with pride to the fact that she always kept her own last name. The people of Seguin knew her as "Amadita"; we (her great-grandchildren) knew her as "Mamadita." I can still remember her sitting on a large mission-style chair; she wore long skirts that nearly reached the floor and beautiful full blouses buttoned up to her neck. She also wore laced high-top shoes and thick cotton stockings. Her gray hair was always in a *chongo* (bun), and she wore wire-rimmed glasses for reading. I remember her being as wide as she was tall, and her most prominent feature was her nose, which was large, wrinkled, and curled—almost like a beak.

Some say that she was an Indian; that she was an Apache from the plains of south central Texas. We do not know for sure, but she always slept with a hatchet and a shotgun by her bed. We never asked why, but we wondered if maybe this was just her "Indian way." The story goes that one time when she was preparing chicken for dinner she accidentally cut off one of her fingers; they say that she just picked up her detached finger, reattached and bandaged it herself, and kept right on killing chickens, never missing a beat.

She was well known in Seguin as a *partera* (midwife). She helped to deliver many children in town, including most of my immediate family, cousins, and me. She was also an herbalist, and I remember the front room of her house being full of bottles, herbs, and *remedios* (remedies) that she dispensed on many occasions. I also remember seeing medical books in her library. She was an accomplished cook and at one time ran a restaurant; on other occasions she sold *pan dulce* from her living room.

Mamadita lived on Jones Street on a lot with several structures, a well in the middle of the property, and a large chicken coop off to the side. A fancy outhouse was discreetly situated in the back. I remember she had at least five buildings on her property. There was the *casa grande* (the big house or main house) where she lived by herself. It was L-shaped with a covered porch, and there was a large flower bed at the front of the lot. If you entered her house through the front door, you entered the room that held all the books, *remedios,* and *pan dulce*. Family usually entered through the kitchen, which was in the middle of the house. Her bed was in one of the two bedrooms in the back. The other structures on her property were two-room houses that served as rental property or as temporary housing for family members. Mamadita also owned several lots on Jones Street, which led me to appreciate her entrepreneurial skills and creative ways of earning money in addition to her active practice as a *partera*. The story goes that she buried money on her property, but no one has ever admitted to looking for or finding any.

I remember two characters who lived on Mamadita's property and who were well known in Seguin. One was an Anglo man who rented from her and lived by himself. He was tall and slender, with thick white hair. He always wore a suit and made his living selling Bibles throughout Seguin. We knew him as *el viejo de las Biblias* (the old man with the Bibles). The other man was Tento, a mentally disabled fellow who spent his days sweeping sidewalks and begging for coins in town. He was a friendly, harmless person and was cared for by all who knew him. He always came home with food, candy bars, and empty shoe boxes in which he cut slots for coins. He did not rent; rather, Mamagrande took him in at the request of his sister who could no longer take care of him.

Mamadita spent many hours sitting on her porch, by the back room window, or on her patio. We would stop by her house and visit with her several times a week as we walked to school, and we often ran errands for her. She always had candy or *pan dulce* for us, real treats after a full day at school. The most common errand we ran for Mamadita was going to Elmo's Grocery Store for postage stamps.

Mamadita died in November 1955, when she was eighty-seven and I was twelve. My memories of her death are of the family gathering and especially of the *velorio,* or wake. Family members came from as far away as California and Chicago. I had never seen so many fancy cars west of Guadalupe Street, and they belonged to our relatives! I began to think that maybe those who left Seguin could do well in life, at least better than those of us who stayed behind. The *velorio* was something special. Mamadita's body was brought to the house and placed in the living room. The house remained open day and night for friends, neighbors, and relatives to pay their respects. The light in the living room was never turned off, and someone, usually one of the women dressed in black, stayed with the body at all times.

In the meantime, a family reunion of sorts was taking place in the other parts of the house and out in the gardens and yard. Tables were covered with food, and drinks of all types were flowing. Men smoked outdoors as women cared for babies and children inside. Loud cries and wailing would occasionally be heard coming from the house, signifying the arrival of more relatives. As a twelve-year-old, I could run in and out of the house watching different scenes taking place. It was a sad event, yet it was a fiesta. People went from laughing one minute to crying the next and then to laughing again. Many of the folks reminisced, while others met relatives they had never seen before. For two days and nights there was no concern about when and what to eat or when or where to sleep. It was a nonstop family gathering for mourning, socializing, and meeting new relatives. That was the last time I saw many of those relatives.

Although he died before I was born, Mamadita's husband, Luis, had quite a reputation in the family. He was born October 25, 1855, in Mexico and had been a soldier in the army of Porfirio Díaz, the Mexican dictator. The story goes that my great-grandfather accompanied Díaz on a trip to the United States in 1869 and became ill in San Antonio. He was left behind in San Antonio with strict instructions from General Díaz to return to Mexico on his release from the hospital. But Luis escaped from the hospital and went south of San Antonio to Medina County. There Amada's father hired him to work on a farm. He married my great-grandmother on Christmas Eve 1882, when he was twenty-seven and she was fourteen. He became a shoemaker and made that his lifelong career.

As far as I can tell, Luis was also among the first Protestants in the family on my maternal side. He was a Methodist lay preacher in a small town south of San Antonio and an avid Bible reader. He probably converted to Protestantism around the turn of the century. This was the heyday of Anglo Protestant missionary work among the Mexicans in Texas. However, the story of his conversion has been lost. He died in 1929, at the age of seventy-four, before I was born, but his story is part of my heritage.

Mamadita and Papa Luis initiated the maternal side of the family into the Protestant Church and left a strong legacy of religious identity and commitment to the church. The family remembers them as Protestant pioneers and spiritual ancestors. I remember Mamadita as serious and at times stern; I now wonder if her seriousness was part of the dramatic life changes and pietistic attitudes of first-generation Protestants. I value her memory and owe her much for the religious and cultural heritage that is mine.

Papagrande y Mamagrande

Mamagrande and Papagrande, my maternal grandparents, lived at 800 North Guadalupe Street, only about twenty feet from my parents' house. I was born in their home, and to this day I enjoy going back to it. It consisted of two rooms—a kitchen and a larger room that served as bedroom, living room, and den. I remember the latter room as a special place. It contained family pictures of the Molinas and Gallardos, a horse clock, and a special place for the Bible. The Bible was loved and respected in that home to the extent that no one would ever put anything on top of it. The place where it was kept seemed almost sacred. The Bible held the family story (records of births and special events) and was annotated throughout. Papagrande's Bible is now one of my prized possessions and connections to the Seguin of my childhood.

Papagrande's name was Norberto Molina. He was a stocky fellow with a round, light-complexioned face, green eyes, a thick white mustache, and a bald head. His hair, which encircled the lower part of his head, was snow white, and he wore wire-rimmed glasses for reading. Papagrande was born on June 6, 1869, in La Becerra Ranch, Wells County, Texas. He was a *vaquero* (cowboy) in his younger days and met my grandmother when he and a cousin stopped in Seguin on their way back from a cattle drive to North Texas. After marrying my grandmother, he worked as a tenant farmer outside of Seguin in an area they called *La Paloma Blanca* (the White Dove). Later they moved into town to raise their family.

Papagrande never forgot his *vaquero* days. Occasionally, he would saddle up a horse he kept behind the house in the gravel pit, and he would ride into the yard and out into the street. He would put on his cowboy hat, bandanna, and spurs and seemed ready to drive another herd to the stockyards up north. I remember well the excitement when Papagrande was riding his horse; we would all run out of the house screaming and running after him. After the horses and Papagrande were gone, Mamagrande held on to his large hat, saddle, spurs, and riding gear, probably recalling that it was during a stop on a cattle drive that she met the man we knew as Papagrande.

Papagrande never really left *la vida del rancho* (life on the ranch or farm). On an empty lot on the other side of his house, he cultivated a huge garden where he grew an assortment of vegetables, such as carrots and turnips. There was nothing better than his carrots fresh from the ground. He also raised rabbits and chickens and not merely as a hobby. They were part of our diet as we grew up in Seguin. The only things I remember not liking were the goats, Minnie and Blackie, and the fresh goat milk we were expected to drink. It was warm and foamy and had a strong odor that would quickly wake you up in the morning.

Papagrande was a religious man and a devoted church member. As an infant, he was baptized a Catholic but converted to the

Methodist Church when he married my grandmother. He held several leadership roles in La Trinidad Iglesia Metodista, including president of the official church board. In 1942 he received a Bible as a special gift from the church for his service and leadership. He was an intelligent, self-educated man who read his Bible in Spanish on a daily basis. I remember the day he died. It was June 26, 1951, and I must have been about eight years old. We were at home when word came. As a small child, I could not comprehend death other than that I would never see him again. I cried that day for the first time with the pain of loss. I don't remember the wake or the funeral, only crying that night with my family.

Next to my mother and father, Mamagrande was probably the most influential person in my childhood. She was born on April 19, 1883, in Medina Losayo south of San Antonio. Her name was Isabel Gallardo Molina—Gallardo as the daughter of Mamadita and Molina because she married Papagrande Norberto Molina. Mamagrande was a diminutive, frail, and sickly woman. I remember her wearing laced shoes, long skirts, and long-sleeved blouses buttoned to the neck, even during the summers. Like her mother, Mamadita, Mamagrande also wore thick brown stockings. On sunny days she used a *sombrilla* (parasol) for protection from the sun. When she worked in the yard, she wore a *gorro* (a sunbonnet), which almost completely covered her face, neck, and head. You had to look at her directly from the front to see her face.

Mamagrande loved her plants and flowers and enjoyed keeping her yard as clean as she possibly could. Sweeping the dirt yard and watering it down and dusting her home were daily rituals for her. At that time, Guadalupe Street, like most barrio streets, was not paved and presented a constant challenge to homemakers. Mamagrande also took care of the family plots at the cemetery, especially the graves of Papagrande, Mamadita, and Papá Luis, her father. I still remember her loading up her small red wagon with yard tools, flowers, food, water, and her *gorro* and *sombrilla* and walking across town to clean and maintain the family graves. Sometimes we children went with her and spent most of the day on these cemetery excursions. As I look back, these trips to the cemetery helped me learn much about my family, and I feel a connection with them because of my mamagrande. When I return to that cemetery and visit the graves of distant *abuelos*, *tíos,* and *tías*, I feel the spirit of Mamagrande and the importance of memory and respect that she imparted to us.

Because Mamagrande lived next door to us, she was part of my daily life. When my mother worked or left the house, Mamagrande looked after us. In fact, even when our mother was at home, Mamagrande felt free to supervise us. It was assumed that she had full rights to look over us. Mamagrande believed in spanking, tweaking ears, thumping heads, and using whatever it took to get her message across. Her instruments of discipline included belts, brooms, fly swatters, sticks, or whatever was convenient. One day when we got into trouble for something we had done, we all ran under the house, thinking that she would not be able to find us there. But she did find us. And when she realized that the broom would not reach us, she called out for her shotgun. Knowing that Mamagrande was serious, we all ran out from under the house.

Mamagrande was the spiritual leader of the clan, if there ever was a spiritual leader in all of Seguin. Her religious faith was an important and central part of her life, and she made sure that it was also central in our lives. Church attendance was a required activity for all of us at least three times a week: *Servicios de oración* (prayer meetings) on Thursday night, *escuela dominical* (Sunday School), and *servicio de adoración* (worship services) along with the Sunday night *servicio*. Not going to church was never an option. She walked us across Guadalupe Street and across town to church every Sunday regardless of the weather. The most embarrassing experience we could have was to be disciplined by Mamagrande during church; we felt the firmness of her hand on our heads, and she would have us sit next to her for the rest of the service.

Daily prayer and Bible reading were essential elements of Mamagrande's spiritual and religious life. Kneeling for prayer seemed like an eternity, certainly more than we thought our bony knees could stand. I remember peeking at her during her prayers and seeing her covering her eyes with a handkerchief, tears streaming down her face. Just when we thought she might be finishing her prayers, she would sigh deeply and continue, and we then prepared ourselves for another long period of prayer. No meal was eaten without her prayer and blessing. Her prayers at mealtime usually involved recalling all members of the extended family by name, liberally using her handkerchief, and deep sighing throughout.

Mamagrande's daily language, like that of many in the Hispanic community of her generation, was imbued with religious terms and thoughts. For example, when we indicated we were going to do something or we told her we would see her later, she would always respond, *"Si Dios quiere"* (God willing) or *"Si es la voluntad de Dios"* (If it is God's will). God was always *"Diosito,"* and Jesus was referred to as *"El Señor."* *"Si Dios es servido"* (If God is served) was another popular phrase of hers, and was said to remind us that if we served God we would be granted our wishes.

Life with Mamagrande also involved religious and spiritual instruction. In addition to her prayers at mealtime and mandatory church attendance, she also taught us to pray *El Padre Nuestro* (the Lord's Prayer) and to recite *El Credo Apostólico* (the Apostles' Creed). She taught us to memorize Bible verses and to sing hymns. For her, religion was not simply going to church; it was a way of life. The daily spiritual disciplines were central to her everyday life, and children were never too young to learn.

Mamagrande eventually went to live with Mamadita during Mamadita's last days. After Mamadita died, Mamagrande sold my father her house and moved into Tía Chavela's house on Dolly Street, where she lived until her death on July 14, 1961. When I think of my religious faith and spiritual journey, I gratefully remember Mamagrande, her firm hand, her prayers, her love of the Bible, and walking to church with her. She played an important role in grounding my family in the church and in our religious faith. Her notions of how the Christian life was to be lived made a deep impression on me. Her faith was a daily source of strength and hope. Critical and even daily decisions were made in prayer and were guided by her sense of God's presence and guidance. Her theology and religious life were formative and important influences and continue to inspire me today.

Los Maldonados:
Papá Samuel and Mamá Emma

Being a Maldonado was always important to me. We were the only Maldonados in Seguin. In one way or another, everyone in Seguin with that name was related. So I thought that everyone in the world named Maldonado would have to be related to us. Whenever we heard the name on TV or saw it in print, we got excited and tried to figure out how we were related. After all, being Maldonado was very special.

Being a Maldonado in Seguin was to be part of *los Maldonados de Seguin.* The two elders of the family were my grandfather Samuel Maldonado and his nephew, Porfirio Maldonado. Porfirio had two children, Sarah and Eliseo, who eventually moved to San Antonio. My grandfather Samuel and his wife, Emma Maldonado, had three sons and three daughters: David, Florinda, Elvira, Bernabe, Elida, and Sammy. Each had several children, and they all identified themselves as members of los Maldonados, including those with other surnames. Whether Hernández, Téllez, or Camarillo, they were still Maldonado.

My grandfather was born on October 24, 1885, in Wilson County, Texas, to Bernabe Maldonado and Diega Escamilla Maldonado. Papá Samuel was a stocky man with a ready wit and easy laughter. He had a band of white hair encircling his shiny bald head, over which he combed a few strands of gray hair. I remember he wore khaki pants and shirt and always a hat, straw in the summer and felt in the winter. He wore wire-rimmed glasses, as was the style at the time. I don't remember how he got the name Papá Samuel, but it was a name by which he was known to the whole Maldonado clan.

Papá Samuel lived on Aguila Street, a one-block-long street across town from us in an interesting part of Seguin; this was a neighborhood that included Mexicans, blacks, and some Anglos. My grandparents lived in a wooden frame house with a living room that was rarely used, two bedrooms, and a large kitchen through which we entered and where we usually did our visiting. The most outstanding feature of the house, as I recall, was the backyard, where there was a dirt patio surrounded by a concrete walk and a large tool shed off to the side. Two large pecan trees shaded the entire patio. Beyond the shed were several pear and peach trees that were off-limits to us until the right time of the year. The patio was central for family, friends, and neighbors and was especially important for Saturday afternoon domino games.

La casa de Papá Samuel and Mamá Emma was where we gathered after church on Christmas Eve and New Year's Eve. These evenings were great festive occasions. The kitchen table was covered with stacks of hot tortillas, bowls of steaming *frijoles*, chile con carne, and plenty of rice. Stacks of *pan dulce*, especially *pan de juevo, bunuelos*, and *empanadas de calabaza,* were laid out on the countertops. The tamales were kept hot in a big pan on the stovetop and were constantly being replenished. The women usually kept the kitchen going, making sure that everyone had more than enough to eat. The men sat in the living room, while the kids ran around from room to room. Sometimes my cousin Neto would dance for us, or Papá Samuel would show us his accordion. It was an evening of fiesta as we enjoyed Mexican food, visiting with *familia*, and just being together. The big event of the night was when Papá Samuel fired his gun at the stroke of midnight, and this also signaled that the festivities were over and it was time to go home.

Papá Samuel had been a tenant farmer in the area around Seguin until he moved into town. He worked farms in Geronimo, McQueeny, and New Berlin, all within a few miles of Seguin. I still recall his talking of *los alemanes* (the Germans) who owned the land. The story goes that he used to play the accordion at Mexican socials and dances on the farms of Guadalupe County. I remember one day he took out his accordion for us kids to see and to touch, but I never heard him play it.

One of the greatest thrills of my childhood was realizing that Papá Samuel was the custodian at Juan N. Seguin Elementary School, which all of my siblings and I attended. I could actually see my grandfather every day of the week at school. At school Papá Samuel was known simply as "Sam." He always wore a large key chain on his belt, and he had his own office, actually a large closet, where I went during lunch break to see him, so I knew he was an important man. He often found marbles on the school grounds and kept them for me. He also kept my personal marbles so I would not lose them. We shared many laughs in his "office."

I must have been in high school when Papá Samuel retired. One of his favorite daily routines after he retired was visiting with his friends on the corner of Austin and Court streets near the county courthouse. It so happened that I worked across the street in a department store, and I could look out the door and see Papá Samuel again every day. I could hear him and see him laughing and carrying on with his friends. Because he had been the custodian at the elementary school, all the Latinos in town knew him. He was a popular man in town.

Papá Samuel died in September of my freshman year in college. He died in our parents' house on Guadalupe Street during a hurricane that threatened Seguin. He had sought refuge in our house and while there had a stroke. When my parents called to tell me of his death, they said that they understood I could not leave my studies to come to the funeral. But I knew I could not stay away. Without telling them, I flew from El Paso to Seguin for the funeral. I can still hear the murmurs as I walked into the memorial service and went straight to the front to view Papá Samuel's body. I had never seen him sick, sad, or angry. And today I still remember him as the happy fellow others knew as "Sam," as the jovial and talkative friend on the corner by the courthouse, and as the man I loved.

Emma Suttles Maldonado was my paternal grandmother; we all called her Mamá Emma. She was born on November 22, 1891, in Guadalupe County, Texas, to Jasper Suttles and Petra Ramírez Suttles. It was natural that we would call her Mamá Emma, just as we called my grandfather Papá Samuel. According to my father, Mamá Emma was half Hispanic and half English, although I knew her as a Spanish-speaking Hispanic. I never heard her speak English. She never talked about her ethnic background as anything other than *mejicana*. However, my father talked about his maternal grandfather, Jasper Suttles, as an old bearded Englishman who would take him from the farm into town on his horse-drawn wagon. According to my father, his grandfather Jasper came to Texas through Mississippi, met Petra, my great-grandmother, and learned to speak Spanish, although he spoke it with an English accent. They were married on October 10, 1886, in Bexar County, Texas. He adapted to the Mexican people and lived as a *Mejicano*.

On her Hispanic side, Mamá Emma came from the Ramírez family, which was quite active in the Mexican Methodist community in Seguin. Mamá Emma was a small, thin woman. She wore wire-rimmed glasses and had her hair in a *chongo*. Like Papá

Samuel, Mamá Emma had an easy laugh and a light attitude. She was fun to be around because of her sense of humor. Mamá Emma used to crochet and also made three-dimensional decorative stars, or *castillos,* that were covered with patchwork. She also made what we called *pan de ule* (rubber bread). These were round flat cakes with air holes, similar to pancakes. We ate them like pastry. We all assumed that they were part of our *cultura.* Many years later my wife and I were in Victoria, British Columbia, and stopped for tea and crumpets. To my great surprise the crumpets were Mamá Emma's *pan de ule.* Apparently Mama Emma had learned to make them from her English father.

Mamá Emma smoked! She always had her cigarettes handy in her apron pocket. In her earlier days, she rolled her own cigarettes using Bugler tobacco. I still remember the little empty tobacco bags in which I kept my marbles. I think she also enjoyed an occasional beer. Unfortunately, smoking caught up with her. She developed a lengthy, terminal case of emphysema. For many months she was bedridden, and her daughter "Lala" (Elida) took care of her until her death. I think Mamá Emma probably smoked until her last days.

Because Mamagrande and Papagrande, my maternal grandparents, died when I was very young, Papá Samuel and Mamá Emma, my paternal grandparents, were the ones I remember best and with whom I had more interaction. Mamagrande and Papagrande were the sources of my religious and spiritual grounding; Mamá Emma and Papá Samuel were more influential in my Hispanic cultural development. They taught me how to laugh and to celebrate. In their home I heard laughter and Mexican music and I learned to play dominoes and checkers. They taught me to tell a good story. Their home was always a place for friends and neighbors. To them, life was fiesta. There was always something to celebrate—birthdays, Christmas, New Year's, or whatever. Life, family, and friends were affirmed as good and worthy of celebration. When I remember Papá Samuel and Mamá Emma, a smile comes to my face.

Mi Papá

How can I begin to tell the story of my father, especially since he is gone? No matter how much I say about him, there is much that is left out. I am sure that my brother and sisters have much more to say, and they may remember differently. Nonetheless, this is a glimpse of all that I remember of my father and carry with me.

My father was David Maldonado. We called him "Apa," probably a shortened form of Papá. When speaking about him to others we would use the term *"mi papá,"* but within the family and especially in conversing with him it was always "Apa." I remember Apa as a strong, handsome man who worked every day of his adult life until he retired. He was of medium height and build. He wore round wire-rimmed glasses, and he always wore a hat. He used to say that a man always wore a hat. He had a ruddy complexion, and his skin was weathered from working long hours in the sun; as a kid he was called *El Güero*. Apa had beautiful wavy hair that grayed at the temples later in life, blue eyes, and a ready smile. He had big strong hands that would engulf mine. His arms were thick and strong; I remember hanging from them as a small kid.

Apa always wore khaki pants and a blue denim work shirt. Since he worked outdoors most of his life, this was his daily attire. Even in summer he wore long-sleeved denim shirts. For thirty years, Apa worked at the Max Starke Municipal Golf Course in Seguin. He was a greens keeper, and his day began at dawn, long before the golfers teed off. He had to have the greens mowed and ready when the first golfers of the day arrived. As a young child, I remember the excitement I felt when he let me join him for a day at the golf course. The morning was still dark and the grass wet from the morning dew. Most people were still asleep, and here we were on our way to work.

I was very impressed with Apa's huge mowing machines. They were kept in a warehouse hidden in the park but close to the river. The warehouse contained his machines, tools, cans of strange fluids, bags of golf balls, and broken golf clubs; everything smelled like oil, gas, and grass combined. I would follow Apa as he prepared his machine and started out toward the golf course. He walked every green and in between the greens. As he walked back and forth, I walked patiently behind him or played on the side of the green. I did not play a round of golf until I was in my mid-twenties. And today, when I play golf and see the workers, I always remember my dad in his khaki pants, blue denim shirt, and straw hat, the old warehouse, his big machines, and his walking all day long.

Apa was born on October 6, 1908, not far from Seguin in Guadalupe County, and spent his early years doing farmwork as the eldest son of a tenant farmer. Many times he told us of plowing with a team of mules, and of life *en el rancho*. He did not necessarily love it, but he had many good stories to tell about his life on the farm. Some of my favorites were the ones about how he and the other kids used to scare each other at night with whistle sounds and white sheets. His formal education began in a rural schoolhouse in New Berlin; I remember picnicking with our family there and Apa telling his stories. He completed the eighth grade at the Seguin Mexican School, later known as Juan N. Seguin Elementary School, which his children attended later on.

My father met my mother, Anita Molina, in church, at La Trinidad Iglesia Metodista in Seguin. My mother's parents, Norberto and Isabel Molina, were pillars of the church; the Maldonados, Samuel and Emma, were also active members. Mamá Emma's family (whose name was Ramírez) was also active in the church. Apa was nine years older than my mother and was not a popular suitor with Papagrande, my mother's father, because of their age difference and also because Apa had been married before. His first wife died soon after their marriage. Papagrande refused to allow my future parents to see each other, and my dad had to write secret letters to my mother to communicate with her. An approved marriage was out of the question. Church was the only place they could see each other, and even there it was not condoned.

So my father and mother eloped! And they did so from the church. The story is that they arranged for my mother to leave the church during services and run away with my father. They were married in the home of a relative who lived on a farm outside Seguin. The elopement and the way in which they did it were considered a great insult, and my mother's parents were outraged and deeply hurt. Papagrande refused to see them or allow them to come back for his blessing.

My parents left Seguin and moved to Robstown, where my dad worked at a relative's gas station. It was the depression and the gas station soon closed. My parents returned to Seguin only after my mother's parents agreed to receive them. But before that could occur, they were required to go to the church altar and pray for forgiveness. This agreement was arranged through the mediation of the Methodist pastor. He, along with my father and his father, went to Papagrande's house to arrange for a reconciliation. My grandfather insisted that my parents meet them at the church during a Thursday evening prayer service. The pastor called my parents to the altar and prayed with them. After the service they all went to my mother's parents' home for the first time. Eventually, my father and grandfather became great friends, partners, and neighbors.

On returning to Seguin, Apa worked for the Works Progress Administration (WPA). One of the WPA projects nearby was a bridge on Highway 68 between Seguin and San Antonio. The bridge still stands near Randolph Air Force Base. My dad worked on that bridge and was always proud to tell me whenever we crossed it on our way to San Antonio that he helped to build it. As soon as a job in town became available for him, he took it. The job was working for the natural gas company.

My father's, and thus our family's, first mode of transportation was a bicycle that he cared for with pride. I remember it well. It had wide tires, shiny fenders, and a big wire basket in front of the handlebars. My biggest thrill was riding with him; my place was on the handlebars. We rode together to the barbershop, Mamá Emma's, and downtown. I remember one Saturday afternoon after we had gotten our haircuts at Sepúlveda's on Court Street, we went to the Ramírez Grocery Store, bought some Big Red soft drinks, and sat on the curb to drink our rewards. To our great joy we found five or six coins in nickels and quarters right by the curb. I still dream of that event. Each time I find a coin I cannot help but think of sitting on that curb in Seguin with my dad with a cold Big Red in my hand.

Apa's first car was a 1936 Chevrolet that he bought from my uncle Berna. It was a beige four-door sedan with a stick shift and starter on the floor, two panel front windows, and a trunk with the door perpendicular to the ground. The day he brought the car home, we all ran out to see it, and just as quickly, we made it our playground. We spent many hours playing inside the car, pretending we were driving. We also used the car as a slide and jungle gym. This was the car in which I began to think of driving and in which I took my first drive.

Apa was a joker and a great storyteller. During the summer months, we spent many evenings sitting outside in the backyard eating fresh-cut watermelon. With *tíos y tías* and at least one grandparent in attendance, we would play *las escondidas* or catch lightning bugs and smear them on our arms and faces. As the evening turned dark, we joined the adults as they listened to stories and *pláticas*, usually about relatives or experiences on the farm. Our favorite stories were scary ghost stories of *la llorona* (the weeping woman), sightings of *el diablo* (the devil), and speculation about the end of the world. These stories usually kept us close to our parents; we were too afraid to even go to the bathroom. After consuming the watermelon and not wanting to leave because of the stories, there were many bed-wetting accidents during the night.

My father often recounted the story of my birth. He was working for the gas company, and the morning after I was born he was down in a deep ditch when word came to him that I was very sick. He ran home and found that I was dehydrated and had a high fever. Dr. Hugh Davis, who with the assistance of Mamadita delivered me, told my father, "Don't let that boy die." I was the first male in my family and thus my birth was a significant event for my parents. They say I survived because they constantly kept a bottle of water in my mouth to rehydrate me. Whenever my father told me that story, tears would come to his eyes and his voice would crack.

On March 29, 1943, not long after I was born, my father took the job as a greens keeper. This was the job he held for thirty years and as far back as I can remember. When he retired on September 30, 1963, the city council gave him a watch with his name on it that he wore with great pride; before he died, he gave it to me. It is a priceless possession. After his retirement, Apa lived for ten years. He continued to enjoy working outdoors, and our yard became a garden under his watchful care. He loved his pecan trees and the plants surrounding the house. He spent a lot of time sitting outdoors in conversation with his friends and neighbors. He and Tío Porfirio spent many hours talking, debating religion, and just reflecting together.

Mi papá was as instrumental in my life as any father could possibly be. He was the model of hard work, discipline, familial obligation, respect, and humor. But his social views have probably had more impact on me than anything else. How he saw and interpreted the world around him helped me to see and understand my world from the perspective of a poor workingman. My father was a social critic. He was intimately aware of injustice in Seguin and in his life. He was keenly aware of the oppression of the poor by the rich. He would observe, *"Los ricos son ricos sobre las espaldas de los pobres"* (The rich are rich on the backs of the poor), or *"Se hicieron ricos con nosotros"* (They became rich at our expense). He was especially critical of the landowners who oppressed poor tenant farmers, especially the German farmers who ill-treated Mexican-American workers. He would point out to me how, in Seguin, Anglos would get and have, while Mexican-Americans were left out and had not. He remembered stories of lynchings and other violence committed against blacks and Mexicans. He had a sense of social rage, which he controlled, but it was undeniably there.

My father was not impressed by wealth or power. He mistrusted the wealthy and took the words of politicians lightly. He did not believe everything he read and questioned the way things were, especially for the poor. On the other hand, his treasure was his family and his friends. He led a simple life and enjoyed simple things like flowers, good conversation, and home-cooked meals. He appreciated a beautiful day in which to work, and a warm evening to enjoy under the trees with family and friends.

I never saw my dad drink alcohol, although I understand that in his younger days he enjoyed a drink or two. Smoking hand-rolled cigarettes made from Prince Albert tobacco was his only vice. That he worked seven days a week for most of our lives to provide for us was a great lesson to me. He denied himself so that our needs could be met. He worked for thirty years at the same job, and in doing so, he taught me about dedication and hard work. Having come through the Great Depression, he was conservative in his finances, and so we lived in the same house all of our lives. Although he worked for low wages, he managed to save money and left no unusual bills.

My father was a religious man. Although he could not attend church on Sunday mornings because of his job, he was in church every Sunday evening. He had a religious worldview and was deeply spiritual in his own way. He enjoyed quizzing the ministers about biblical and theological issues, to the point that they were eager to escape. His public prayers were infrequent but moving. He possessed a strong religious faith. His life was simple and honest.

Dad died in June 1984 in Seguin. He did not deserve the slow and painful death he experienced as a consequence of pancreatic cancer. His death was hard on all of us. Signing papers in order for his body to be removed was one of the hardest things I have ever done. However, I have developed a deep sense of joy, gratitude, and especially pride in having had him as *mi papá*.

Mi Mamá

My mother's has been an incredible journey rooted in Seguin, her family, and her deep religious faith and active involvement in the church. She was born on November 8, 1916, in Seguin on Jones Street at Mamadita's house. Mamadita served as *partera*. My mother, Anita, was one of nine children born to Norberto and Isabel Gallardo de Molina. Her family's struggles to keep their children alive beyond childhood were not uncommon among Hispanic families in the early 1900s. Only five of the nine siblings lived beyond infancy: Anita, Adelfa, Isabel, Abel, and Norberto. Adelfa and Abel died of pneumonia—Abel, as a young man of twenty-two, Adelfa as a child. Norberto, Isabel, and my mother have lived to older age. There was one infant brother whom mother remembers, Alejandro, who died at the age of six months, probably also of pneumonia.

Amá, as we called her, spent the first thirteen years of her life *en el rancho* in the Paloma Blanca, outside of Seguin. A small structure from that farm still stands on the outskirts of town on Farm Road 68 across from the Cementerio Santo Tomás. When my mother lived there, the farm consisted of a cluster of houses where Mamadita's extended family lived. It was while she lived on this farm that Mother began school. Like the rest of the Mexican-Americans in the Seguin area, she attended Juan N. Seguin Elementary School, which was four miles from her home. Mother, along with her two brothers and Adelfa, walked those four miles to school and back home. But before Mother could complete her first year of school, Adelfa died. Mother was kept at home to help with the daily chores. She did not return to school until she was a teenager, when she attended night classes at Juan N. Seguin Elementary; it was then that she learned some English.

When Mother was in her early teens, her grandfather Luis died, and she and her family moved to Crystal City, Texas, where they worked in the fields during the day and operated a restaurant in the evenings. Mother worked in the restaurant kitchen. In the middle of the depression, the family decided to move back to Seguin. They returned to Jones Street when Mother was fifteen or sixteen.

Returning to Seguin also involved returning to the church where my mother's family had been active members. The Maldonados (my dad's family) were also an active church family, and Mother had known our father, David, through the church most of her life. Mother was sixteen and Dad was twenty-five years old when she returned to Seguin. But Dad was a widower then; his young wife had died. In fact, Mother was an attendant at the young woman's funeral. Mom and Dad became interested in each other, but Papagrande strongly opposed their courtship. He did not allow them to speak to each other or to exchange letters. He even had Mother sleep on the floor next to their bed so that he could keep an eye on her. It was through cousins and secret letters or in church that my parents could communicate. Mother recalls that on Sundays when her family would walk to church, she and her cousins would try to walk a short distance ahead of her parents so they could talk about Dad. If they got too far ahead, her parents would call them back. On one such occasion, Dad waited for them and joined them on the walk to church. Papagrande quickly sped up, got between the sweethearts, and made conversation with my future father to keep him from talking to Mother.

Mother and Dad made plans to marry anyway and agreed to elope from church on Thursday night, June 26, 1935. As planned, they sneaked out of church during prayer time. Dad had made arrangements for a friend to have a car ready; this friend's brother later became my *padrino* (godfather). Although they had not gotten a marriage license, my parents found Judge Williams, a justice of the peace in Wilson County, who married them with the understanding that the next day the young couple would get a marriage license. So they got married and had a reception that evening at the house of one of Dad's cousins, Candida Rodriguez, outside of Seguin. They served hot chocolate, cookies, and cake. Sadly, neither my dad's nor my mother's immediate family attended the wedding or the reception. Mom was seventeen and Dad was twenty-six when they got married. Mother was finally allowed to visit her parents about four months after she and my dad were married.

This story of our parents' courtship and first step as a married couple illustrates the strict upbringing of young women at that time, especially as they approached marriage age. Parents were concerned with family honor, respect, proper procedures, and especially acknowledgment of their position of authority. It was important that young people receive their parents' blessings in important decisions such as marriage. My parents' story also illustrates the important role of the church in the social lives of families and individuals.

Early in their marriage my parents lived with both sets of in-laws in and around Seguin. They lived for a short time in Robstown. But for most of their marriage, they lived in Seguin. The first and only home they owned was at 802 North Guadalupe Street, where my siblings and I grew up. When I was about six years old, Mother started to work outside the home. For many years she cleaned houses and took care of other people's children while our grandmother took care of us. Later, I recall her working at the Frito Lay Company canning tamales and other Mexican food; she worked there for three years. When the company left Seguin, Mother got a job at the local cleaners, where her work included doing alterations. While she was working at the cleaners, the manager of Seguin Leader Department Store recruited her to do alterations. Mother worked for Seguin Leader for nearly twelve years.

I remember Mother getting up to feed and see my dad off to work around 5:30 in the morning. She would then get us up, feed us, and get us ready for school, and then she would walk up Guadalupe Street to work downtown at the store. She worked six days a week from 8:00 A.M. to 6:00 P.M. Where she got her energy, I do not know. It was during this time that Mamagrande took care of us. My older sisters were also left in charge of us after school and on Saturdays.

For most of her life, Mother was a petite woman with curly dark hair. Her eyes were bright, and she had a shy smile. She was usually a serious person with much on her mind and schedule. Some would say that she was always in a hurry. I can still see her walking rapidly with her big purse under her arm. She learned to drive a car later in life, and when Dad bought the second car, she was the primary driver for the family, including trips out of town such as to the coast or to San Antonio. On many occasions, Dad sat in the backseat while Mother drove.

In a way, Mother was the dreamer and spiritual force of the family. She wanted her children to have what she never had, and she made that possible. Somehow she managed to buy us new clothes every fall for school, special church outfits for Easter and Christmas, a new set of encyclopedias, tennis rackets, piano lessons, and something special when she could. At times she had to argue with Dad over these expenses, but she bought them anyway. Her family was her joy.

Mother was happiest when she was surrounded by family. The Christmas season was probably the high point of her year. She would buy a special present for each one of us, and a Christmas tree was an unbroken tradition. On Christmas Eve we attended church and returned home for the opening of gifts and a feast of tamales and chile con carne. She beamed with her biggest smile of the year on this night. She gave special attention to how each one of us responded to her gifts and always explained why she bought each one.

After her family, the church was probably the next love in her life, and it was her second family. She was raised in the church and always took great pride in her roots. She made sure that we were also grounded in the church. Church attendance was a family way of life; it was not an option but just what we did. When we were young, she and her mother worked together to get us ready for church and walked us there. She especially wanted us to dress with respect for church; she made dresses for the girls and bought the boys special slacks and shoes. When she realized that the church would need a pianist, she encouraged the girls to take piano lessons and saved to buy the family a piano. When asked why she arranged for piano lessons and a piano for her family, her response was that it was for the church. That piano sits in the church fellowship hall today, representing her sacrifice and commitment.

Mother was an active member of the choir and the *Sociedad de Mujeres Metodistas* (Methodist Women's Society) and served on numerous church committees. She cooked and served for church dinners and did whatever she could to help. It was her life. Her closest friends have been people she met at church. For me, church means seeing my mother there and hearing her distinctive voice singing among the many voices of the congregation.

Mother was and continues to be a *servidora* (servant, helper). She finds pleasure and great satisfaction in helping others. Whether hosting people with *pan mejicano* and *café*, calling on the sick and elderly, or simply expressing her care, she always seeks to make people feel loved. When she was a young retiree she was a volunteer with the Retired Senior Volunteer Program and was honored for her service. In the church, she has been a servant all of her life. In the barrio, she has been a caring neighbor. In her family, she has been an endless fountain of love and caring.

Above all, Mother has been the spiritual leader of the family. Her faith and spirituality, especially her way of life, have been sources of strength and guidance for all of us. In a real way, she has become the Mamagrande of today. Her prayers are powerful and moving. When she prays, tears flow from her eyes as well as from the eyes of all gathered around the table or in the room. During prayer she recalls all of her children, grandchildren, and great-grandchildren. Her prayers are prayers of gratitude, of concern for others, and of the wish for strength.

In the midst of my sister Amelia's recent illness and subsequent untimely death, Mother's deep religious faith and personal strength shone through. She was a source of strength for the rest of the family. Throughout the four weeks of sitting and waiting in a hospital visitors' room, with brief visits to the Intensive Care Unit where Amelia lay unconscious and on life support, Mother was faithful and caring. She constantly talked to Mele, wiping her forehead and praying, not knowing whether Amelia could hear or recognize her. What was important to Mother was that she was caring for Mele. Mother never gave up hope. Nonetheless, it was painful to Mother to lose a daughter. "I never expected that one of my children would die before I did. I would rather die first," were her expressions of pain. Yet her faith sustained her and she entrusted Amelia to God's hands. *"Que se haga la voluntad de Dios"* (May God's will be done) was her ultimate expression of faith.

Mom has refused to leave the house she has known as her home since she married as a young girl. She belongs in that house. It is difficult to imagine that house without her and life without her. She has been a powerful formative force in my life. Her roots in Seguin, her love of family, her religious faith, and her life in the church have left a major stamp on my life. Her dreams and hopes for a better life shaped mine.

Mis Padrinos

Padrinos (godparents) are very important people for Latino children and parents. They are a lifelong presence and play important roles in the lives of the child and the parents from the moment of the child's baptism, which is usually during infancy. *Padrinos* are people selected by the parents to serve as witnesses of the baptism ceremony and to serve as *compadres* (co-parents) to the child. The tradition has been that if the parents died while the child was still a minor, the *padrinos* were expected to raise the child as their own. *Padrinos* could be relatives or friends. However, once the baptism event takes place, they become *compadres* and *comadres* (co-fathers and co-mothers) for life.

As *compadres,* they develop close relations with the parents. Both sets of adults refer to each other as *comadre* or *compadre*. The *compadres'* birthdays are celebrated together, and gifts are exchanged during special holidays. Frequent visits to each other's homes and exchange of personal favors are expected. Such was the case with my *padrinos*, Francisco and Paula Tovar. In Seguin, they were known as Kiko and Paulita. They lived across the street from Mamadita and were active members of our church. Kiko was a stocky, bronzed man with a contagious laugh and constant cough. He would laugh so hard that you thought he was going to choke. My *madrina* (godmother), Paulita, was a quiet woman of short stature, shy but quick to laugh. I believe that my *padrino,* Kiko, was the church treasurer for many years, because I remember seeing him in the church office counting the offering. My *padrino* worked at the slaughterhouse and many times would stop by our house to give my father *lengua, sesos, y tripas* (tongue, brains, and tripe) and other delicacies. My *madrina* continues to be a close friend of my mother's and is a frequent visitor in her home to this day. I have enjoyed watching the warm relationship between these two couples and the joy and laughter they share as *compadres* and *comadres.*

As the child whose baptism placed me at the center of this *compadrazgo* relationship, I learned the importance of my *padrinos* and the ways I was to interact with them. I was taught to refer to them always as Padrino and Madrina and to show them the respect one shows a parent. There also were benefits to enjoy as an *hijado* (godchild). I was like an *hijo* to my *padrinos*. *Hijado* literally means "one who is made a son." I received special birthday and Christmas gifts from them, and I was also expected to reciprocate. As I got older, I was expected to visit their home and pay my respects. My *padrino* died many years ago. I visited his grave at Cementerio Santo Tomás during a recent visit to Seguin. To this day I value his caring attentiveness to my well-being; I especially cherish his great sense of humor. My *madrina* still lives on Jones Street in Seguin, and I enjoy her warm smile and quick laughter whenever I see her.

My *padrinos* were simple people who worked hard and loved the church. They had no children of their own (they later adopted a son), so they treated me royally. Although they had little formal education, they taught me great lessons through their kindness, presence, and service in the church and deep and loyal friendship with my parents.

The *compadrazgo* system is a central social practice among Mexican-Americans. It expands the extended family and joins families, especially adult couples, for life. It also provided me with an important intergenerational link. Conversations and visits with my *padrinos* opened the door for many hours of sharing, inquiry, and *consejos* (counsel). They were indeed my second parents and were an integral part of my formative years in Seguin.

Los Sábados

Saturdays were special days for children in my generation—not only because it meant no school and we could sleep late, but because they were filled with special events and surprises. Something always happened on Saturdays. I remember that it was the day when my father worked only until noon. He would come home by lunchtime, and in the afternoon we would do something special together. One of those Saturday events was going to Mamá Emma's house. My father visited his parents every week without fail, usually on Saturdays, and I got to tag along. The story goes that I liked to sit on a brick that Mamá Emma had covered with cloth and used as a doorstop. Our mode of transportation at that time was my father's bicycle, and I used to think I was the luckiest kid in Seguin because I was able to ride in the basket as my father rode his bike.

Saturday afternoons at Mamá Emma's house were festive occasions. There were always a number of people there, including Mamá Emma, Papá Samuel, Tío Berna, Sammy, Lala, and Tía Elvira, and a number of Maldonado grandchildren. The neighbors would drop by while the family sat around in the backyard or in the kitchen. Needless to say, there were always several conversations going on at once, and bursts of laughter were often heard throughout the house. Mamá Emma's house was fun, and she always had something special for me to drink.

Visits to Mamá Emma's house usually involved an afternoon of dominoes. I spent many hours standing by my dad carefully watching his hand as he played dominoes with his father, brothers, and neighbors. I marveled at how Apa, Papá Samuel, and my *tíos* played the game. Somehow they could tell who had what and why they were playing particular "rocks." They were also counters, and each was able to tell you how many aces, blanks, or numbers were on the table, how many were out, and who probably had them. It was a game of strategy, bluffing, teasing, and challenges. It was especially fun to walk around the table and watch them develop their game strategies. The biggest thrill was when I was invited to join the table to play, usually when a player had to leave temporarily; I was an older child by then.

In addition to the dominoes and scoring pad, the domino table was usually covered with beer cans and clouded with cigarette smoke. Papá Samuel was an occasional drinker and smoker, but my uncles were nonstop smokers and drank throughout the games. Making smoke rings and other shapes was a side game. My grandmother and aunts gladly provided an unending supply of beer. I never saw my father drink a beer, but he joined in the smoking. Smoking was his *vicio* (vice).

Another Saturday event with my dad was the monthly trip to the barbershop. There were two shops that served Mexican-Americans in Seguin at that time, but the main one was Sepúlveda's on Court

Street. It was a simple shop with four big barber chairs and a long mirrored wall with about eight chairs lined up against the wall for waiting customers. Sepúlveda's barbershop was one of the town's central crossroads for Mexican-Americans, and almost every man and boy eventually went there for a haircut. I can recall how my haircuts mirrored my growth and development. At the beginning, Dad and I rode his bike to González's barbershop, where I was usually seated on a board that was placed on top of the armrests of the barber chair. My father determined my haircut style—usually a very short cut with the sides practically shaved but with enough left on top for the hair to be shaped with a part on the left side. A major transition for me was when I no longer needed the booster chair; by that time we were riding in Dad's green 1953 Chevy. The final stage was when Mr. Sepúlveda asked me how *I* wanted him to cut my hair.

Sitting to the side watching my dad getting his hair cut and joking with Mr. Sepúlveda and everyone who entered the shop were great Saturday moments. I could not figure out how my dad knew so many people in Seguin, but I certainly enjoyed his humor and being part of the whole scene. *"¿Oye, David, dónde dejaste la bicicleta?"* ("Hey, David, where did you leave your bicycle?") *"¿Mira, Pedro, todavía vives?"* ("Hey, Pedro, are you still alive?") I learned that men loved to talk and that the barbershop was an ongoing public stage for playing and teasing, as well as a central place for male gossip, news, and exchange of information.

Saturdays were special. They involved doing things with my father whom I had seen very little during the week. Those moments together were and still are important to me. They gave me time with my dad but also opportunities to observe him as a member of his family and the Latino community. I enjoyed his sense of humor and his playful interactions with friends and neighbors, and I especially appreciated his respect and love for his own parents.

Saturdays were also days for buying the groceries. I never went to buy the groceries, but they are memorable because of the surprises (*el pilón*) that were usually stuffed in the bags of food.

The routine was simple. Someone from the family went to Elmo's Grocery Store on Guadalupe Street with a list. Elmo filled the order and delivered it himself in his panel truck, since we did not yet have a car. The surprise was the candy that Elmo would freely tuck in as a gift to us. As soon as he would leave, all of us children would run to the bags and take out the groceries as fast as we possibly could searching for our treats. Apparently he knew our economic situation and valued our business. It was our *pilón,* and it made our day.

Saturdays were also transitional days. They were the time for the mandatory bath and the selection and preparation of clothing for the next day's church activities. Sometimes, it even meant reading your Sunday school lesson in preparation for the next day.

Los Domingos

Sundays meant *iglesia y familia*. The main events of the day were going to church in the morning, followed by a family *comida* (meal) and an afternoon of visiting or hosting *familiares* from across town, from San Antonio, or from the coast. The day started very early because there were seven of us children, five of whom were girls who spent more than their share of time in the bathroom. My father was usually at work, so he never went to church with us on Sunday mornings. But he would be home for *la comida* when we returned from church. My mother and Mamagrande were the ones who made sure that we arrived at church on time, as clean as we could get, and in the best clothes we could afford. Going to church was a special weekly event. It was the only time we dressed up; we had special Sunday shoes and clothing that we didn't wear any other time. My sisters wore high heels, hose, and fancy dresses, many of which were made by my mother, and had their hair specially combed. I vividly remember my mother combing my hair when I was young, not always an easy task for her or for me. I had thick wavy hair and her combing pulled my head all the way to the side while I struggled to keep it upright. She dressed me in matching shirts and pants that she ordered from Sears. As a teenager, I proudly wore suits or sport coats. To wear a tie and coat was a special thing for me. It made me feel grown up and dignified.

The Sunday noon meal was the "formal" meal of the week when the family, still in our Sunday attire, all sat at the table together. The meal was the fanciest of the week, which meant we got to eat white bread. Apa was home from work and had gotten cleaned up by then. As soon as we got home, Ama and the girls would busily put together a big meal and the table would be set. Mamagrande said the prayer with her usual sighs, tears, and wet handkerchief. She would pray for each member of the extended family by name, explain each person's situation to God, and ask for specific divine action. My dad always sat in the same place at the table, and my mother, wearing her trusted apron, sat next to him. Her place was the one closest to the stove, and she would sit down only minutes at a time. She was always hopping up to get more food and make sure that everyone had what he or she needed. She was the one who served my dad his food.

When we had company for Sunday lunch, the adults sat at the big table while the children ate at a small side table. Company always ate first and had the choice portions. As children from the host family, we ate last. But it was my mother who really ate last. She would insist that everyone else was eating before she began.

La comida de domingo was usually followed by a brief nap or visiting with guests. In those days, relatives or friends did not have telephones to call us before coming over. They just appeared. Many a Sunday we awoke from our naps to find a carload of relatives in the yard arriving to spend the afternoon. We would all jump up to look out the windows to figure out who was there. My mother would go out to welcome the visitors only after determining who they were. If it was winter or a cool day, the guests would enter through the kitchen and sit around the kitchen table to visit. On summer Sundays, the company would be invited to sit outside in the backyard under the big trees. While they were seating themselves, my mother would already be preparing a pot of coffee and setting out a tray of *pan dulce*.

Hosting relatives on Sunday afternoons was a special treat and ritual. We got to meet relatives from Seguin, San Antonio, Beeville, Mathes, Corpus Christi, Chicago, and Laredo. We would sit in a circle, with the best chairs reserved for visitors. They would not be dressed in their Sunday best, but close to it. Thus, it was difficult for us to play as rough as we would have liked. This made the visits somewhat formal. The main activity was conversation, which consisted of bringing everyone up to date on family matters, important events, and relationships. There was a lot of reminiscing, remembering deceased family members, and talking about other relatives. When it was time to leave, it took several attempts or announcements. As gracious hosts, my parents always insisted that visitors stay a little longer, and they would dutifully comply. This went back and forth for at least an hour until the guest finally left. After company left, it was time for a quick *merienda* and preparations for Sunday night church services. My father would go to the evening services with us.

The most notorious visitor was Tío Amado. He and his wife, Matilde, would frequently pay formal visits on Sundays. Because they lived nearby, they would walk over to our house, and we would not know they were coming until Tío Amado was standing at the door, peeking in to see if we were home. Tío Amado would sit at the kitchen table and sip his coffee for hours. Mother, the ever-gracious hostess, would serve empanadas or food from the noon meal. He never said no to food or coffee. After a few hours of visiting, he would begin his usual announcements—

"Bueno, ya nos vamos" (OK, now we're going), to which Mother would respond, *"No, no se vayan tan pronto"* (No, don't leave so soon). She was being polite, but he took her literally, and he would say, *"Bueno, solo un ratito"* (OK, only a little while). At this Mother served another cup and the conversation would continue. After several such announcements, Dad would excuse himself, many of us would leave the kitchen, and Mother was left to entertain Tío Amado and his wife. Only after they left would Dad and the rest of us come out.

No housework was done at home on Sundays, and we were free to enjoy our friends, family, and church. Because we were Protestants, we could not go to the movies on Sundays, much less to a dance. Some would say that we were pietistic. But we felt we were being good Methodists and respecting the day of rest. Sunday was totally devoted to religious and familial activities. Yet it was the most social day of the week for us.

La Iglesia

I was reared in La Trinidad Iglesia Metodista, a small Spanish-language Protestant church that served Mexican-Americans in Seguin and the surrounding area. The church was located across town from our house and two blocks from the center of Seguin. The church building was built in 1864 and originally housed the German Methodist Episcopal Church. In 1905 the Board of Missions of the Methodist Episcopal Church South bought the building and parsonage from the German congregation. The first minister of the congregation was Basilio Soto, who was appointed by La Conferencia Fronteriza Mejicana (Mexican Border Conference). It was the only Hispanic Protestant church in Seguin when I was a young boy, and it played an important role in the religious life of the community. The congregation was developed as a special ministry by and for Mexican-Americans. Thus, it emerged as a separate and autonomous congregation. It shared denominational identity with the African-American Methodist Church and the (Anglo) First Methodist Church in town, but it did not share in any other way in those days.

Pastoral leadership was originally provided through La Conferencia Fronteriza Mexicana and later the Rio Grande Conference of the Methodist Church, a Spanish-language annual conference of that denomination. All the ministers that I remember were Hispanic and lived next door to the church. The ministers made a strong impression on me. They were the only Hispanic leadership models that I knew. Not only were they publicly visible leaders, self-confident, and articulate, they were also models of spiritual strength. They spoke of God, handled the elements of Holy Communion, and presided over important events such as baptisms, weddings, and funerals. Ministers were received in our home with the highest respect; early on, I got the impression that they were special. No one else in our community wore suits and had a title in front of their names.

Reverend Eugenio Vidaurri is the first minister I remember. He was of small stature, but he was a dynamic speaker. He was firm, leaning toward the pietistic, and always wore a tie, even during the hot summers. He was also one of the first Mexican-Americans in town who owned a car. He provided strong leadership and brought structure to the church. He was especially concerned that the congregation be organized according to the Methodist Discipline and polity. It was under his leadership that the church built its modern building. He encouraged me to become involved in the church and gave me many opportunities to participate. I also remember Reverend José Salas. He opened his home to me and allowed me to see the human side of ministers. He enjoyed a good joke and loved to share his boyhood stories. He was also the first minister who was completely bilingual and had a personal library;

this made a huge impression on me. He loved books and challenged me to higher learning.

The Maldonados and Molinas were active families in this particular congregation many years before my generation. Although we did not meet any of the first converts within our family or go through the conversion experience ourselves, we inherited their religious identity and the sense of belonging to a special religious community. It was important to us that we were Methodists! When we looked at old family and church pictures, we saw our grandparents and relatives in the church. It was the family's church, and it was our church.

The first church building that I can recall was the one that was originally the German Methodist Episcopal Church. It was a large white wooden structure with windows that could be opened when it became too hot inside. Large ceiling fans circulated the air directly above our heads. The Goetz Funeral Home contributed fans made of cardboard, with wooden handles, that also helped us keep cool. The building had short double steeples with a double door in the front. When I was a preteen, the congregation built a brick church building on the same spot and moved the old building over to serve as an annex, a Sunday school building, and a fellowship hall.

Church attendance included going to *la escuela dominical* immediately before *el servicio* (the main worship service). For the children, church involved a large dosage of singing *coritos* (gospel songs), memorizing Bible verses, and listening to Bible stories. *"Cristo Me Ama"* (Jesus Loves Me) and *"Dios Hizo los Cielos"* (God Made the Heavens) were popular children's songs. John 3:16 and Psalm 23 were standard biblical passages that we memorized. On special occasions, the children performed during the main worship service, demonstrating our singing abilities and reciting Bible verses. We would all march up to the front in our Sunday best to face the congregation for our performance. Many times, Mary Bustos, the children's Sunday school teacher for many years, would be the dominant voice because we became shy. This was an uncomfortable moment for the children but one of pride for parents and adults. What was difficult about this was sitting in the front for the entire service under the watchful eye of adults, especially the minister's wife, or Maria Bustos, or my grandmother.

As I grew older, attending *los servicios de adoración* became more meaningful and enjoyable. It was in this setting that I learned to read Spanish. While we were prohibited from speaking Spanish during the week in school, in church we were given the opportunity to learn to read in our native language. By following the Bible readings, the words in the hymnals, and listening to the prayers and sermons, I learned Spanish as a formal and powerful form of expression and communication. It was in church that I learned that God was bilingual, that God understood Spanish. I also heard my *abuelitas* and *familia* and others praying, singing, and speaking Spanish with a natural and beautiful joy.

Church was a time and place when *los hermanos y hermanas* (the brothers and sisters of the church) would dress up in their Sunday best. The men who worked with their hands and backs all week wore suits, ties, and polished shoes. During the week they were blue-collar laborers, but on Sunday morning they were Sunday school superintendents, committee chairmen, and leaders in dignified attire and roles. They led worship services with their public prayers and Bible reading. During the week the women were house cleaners or baby-sitters or took in washing and ironing, but on Sunday they wore high heels and hats and sang in the choir. People who during the rest of the week played subordinate roles were transformed on Sunday into dignified, respected leaders of their church.

That small ethnic minority church was a place of belonging for us. It opened its doors to us when access was denied in other places because we were Mexican-Americans. It accepted and affirmed us while other institutions rejected us as well as our Mexican culture. People would say *"Yo soy de la iglesia metodista,"* ("I belong to the Methodist church"). It spoke volumes about our sense of belonging.

Our church represented ownership to Mexican-Americans at a time when we did not own much in the community. It was a special place for us in Seguin. *"Es mi iglesia,"* ("It is my church,") provided insight into the sense of ownership. We owned it and determined what to do in it. There was great pride in the church. The men volunteered to take care of the yard, and the women cleaned the inside. We had fiestas at church that consisted mainly of meals, receptions, and gatherings to celebrate events such as weddings, anniversaries, holidays, and religious days. The pride of ownership was evident and at the core of our small religious community.

The youth met every Sunday and had their own organization and leadership. We learned about Robert's Rules of Order and held positions found in most groups and organizations (president, vice president, secretary, treasurer). Every year we elected officers and celebrated with installation services, and every Sunday we held business meetings and worship services and enjoyed fellowship with other youth. During the winter months, fellowship nights were held on Saturdays, and they consisted of games in the annex along with refreshments. Our favorite games were wink'em, post office, and musical chairs. During the summer months, fellowship nights were usually held on Fridays and involved primarily volleyball and refreshments. Sometimes we invited youth groups from San Marcos, New Braunfels, or Floresville to participate, or we visited them. In essence, the church provided a means for leadership development for Mexican-American youth and space for social life when such opportunities were limited elsewhere.

A special and significant annual event was the conference youth camp for young people from Texas and New Mexico that was held in Kerrville, Texas. Going to camp provided us with many learning and leadership opportunities. We had to plan and prepare for the summer event. This included determining how many of us were going, how much money we would need, and organizing fund-raising activities. We also had to plan how we would get to Kerrville. Preparing for youth camp taught us to make personal plans as well, including what clothing to take, saving money, and packing suitcases and travel kits. I still remember the excitement of planning what I was going to wear each day of camp. I was probably packed a week before I had to leave. But the biggest experience was the actual trip to Kerrville and attending the weeklong camp. Traveling with other young people, eating in a restaurant, and sleeping in a different environment were exciting as well as broadening. But meeting other Mexican-American youth exactly like me—Hispanic and Protestant—was the most significant aspect of youth camp. Just when I thought my family was unique in being Hispanic and Protestant, I met youth from the Valley, San Antonio, Dallas, El Paso, and New Mexico, some from towns that I had never heard of before.

Sunday nights in church were more casual, and the worship service was much more informal as well. There was a great deal of singing, usually of songs selected by the congregation. In addition, there would be a long prayer time at the altar. This included prayers not only by the pastor but also by the members of the congregation. There were prayers of intercession, petition, and repentance as well as for healing and thanksgiving. All of us were expected to kneel, not just those who went to the altar.

Sunday night sermons were evangelistic, and calls to repentance were a common occurrence. The latter included altar calls for those who felt a special personal need, or were moved by the sermon, or were taking a special step toward repentance or conversion. A special part of the service was the *testimonios* (testimonies), in which individuals stood up and shared with the congregation what they considered to be acts of God's blessing, healing, miracles, forgiveness, and goodness, as well as personal experiences of repentance and conversion. *Testimonios* made it possible for both men and women to stand and speak before the congregation. It was empowering for them to have a voice, and their *testimonios* were quite moving and emotional. Tears were not uncommon among those offering their testimonies and among members of the congregation. People spoke from their hearts and shared intimate experiences and concerns. The congregation was attentive, supportive, and responsive, with *"Amen, Gloria a Dios, Gracias a Dios, Asi sea"* (Amen, Glory to God, Thanks be to God, Let it be).

One of the most memorable events of my youth was when I officially joined the church. This occurred when I was fourteen or fifteen. *La Confirmación de Fe y Recepción en la Iglesia* was the public ceremony for youth ready for membership. In essence, it is a ritual in which young people affirm their faith and are welcomed as official members of the church. It is an important event and a highlight of the spring season. I remember several of us wearing new suits or dresses standing in front of the congregation, affirming our faith, and declaring our membership in the church. It was a Sunday morning, one of those rare Sundays when my father was in church. Dad must have taken the day off to be present. At the end of the service we stood at the front of the sanctuary, and the entire congregation walked by greeting and welcoming each of us. It was moving to be greeted by many of the elders of the church whom I respected so much. However, the most memorable moment was when my dad greeted me and said, "Atta boy." I could tell he was proud. Tears were in his eyes, and they immediately came to mine.

The church was a central place in my formative years. *La iglesia metodista* was the church of my parents, grandparents, and great-grandparents; and it was my church. I learned to enjoy it, and I looked forward to its activities. The church provided me with my religious identity, but it also affirmed my culture and instructed me in Spanish. But more than that, the church offered a community of people who cared for me and treated me as their child and later as their brother and peer. They were my *hermanos y hermanas.* We identified with each other and we were family.

Católicos y Protestantes

The Mexican-American community in Seguin was deeply divided between Catholics and Protestants. Most of the Mexican-American townspeople were Roman Catholic and attended Our Lady of Guadalupe Church. Most of the small Protestant population attended La Trinidad Iglesia Metodista. It was clear from the very beginning that these were two very different religious groups who shared mutual ignorance, distrust, and antagonism. This was a period of overt anti-Catholic and anti-Protestant sentiment and activity. There was no such thing as ecumenical dialogue, much less cooperation; you were either a Catholic or a Protestant. To be one was to be against the other.

When I was a young child, especially during my preschool years, conversation about religion was primarily heard in church, or when my *tíos* and *tías* discussed the end of the world when the family gathered in the backyard. The family also talked during thunderstorms about God's anger, and during visits to the cemetery about heaven and hell. I did not associate religion with being Protestant or Catholic during my preschool years. All I knew was that there was a God who was almighty and powerful, who constantly watched over us from above, who caused thunderstorms when angry, and who would some day end the world as we know it. But I also learned about God from my mother and Mamagrande. God, according to my *abuelita,* was the God of the Ten Commandments but also a God of grace and love. God loved us, especially the children. According to my mother, God listens to our prayers and is always close at hand. In church, we learned that God created the world and loved all of us. To me, church meant La Trinidad Iglesia Metodista.

I did not know I was a Protestant or that it was an issue to anyone until my first year at Juan N. Seguin Elementary School. This came to my attention as we passed by Our Lady of Guadalupe Church every day on our walk to school. The church happened to be located next door to Mamadita's house on Jones Street. Every Tuesday afternoon after school, the priest would stand in front of the church and direct the children who were walking home into the church for *doctrina* (catechism). I still recall the first time this happened. The whole scene frightened me. By then, I knew that this church was not the one I attended with my family. We went to another church across town. I made it very clear to the priest and to the other children that I belonged to La Trinidad. I could not have made a worse or stronger statement. I had publicly announced that I was *protestante.*

Those Tuesday afternoons were my introduction to the incredible division between *católicos* and *protestantes*. I had to find another route to my great-grandmother's house on Tuesday afternoons. I became afraid of being caught by the priests, who were ominous figures in their long black skirts, or being caught by *las monjitas* (nuns), who appeared to be peeking out of their strange black habits. I was afraid I would be forced to enter an unfamiliar place. My religious innocence was lost. I began to see my world divided between that which was Catholic and that which was Protestant. I learned that I was Protestant, and because of that, I was different from other *Chicanitos* (Chicano children).

It became known in school that my family was Protestant. Things were never quite the same again. My siblings and I became the targets of many questions and accusations and a great deal of teasing and taunts because of our religious affiliation. We were called *protestantes,* in a disparaging way, as if it were something terrible, ugly, and evil. It felt as though we had a disease, as if we were undesirables or untouchables. Our church was spoken of as the devil's house, and I remember Catholics crossing themselves as they passed by La Trinidad. Catholics told us that we were going to hell because we were Protestants.

I could never understand why Catholics would say such things about our church and about us. What I was taught in church and by my grandmother about God did not seem evil to me. The people whom I saw at church seemed like good people; they included both sides of my family—Mamadita, my *abuelitas, tíos, tías,* and cousins, and my father and mother. How could all of these people whom I knew, trusted, and loved so much be wrong?

Another notion about being Protestant was that we had converted from Catholicism and thus had turned our backs on the Catholic Church. This made no sense to me. I was a fourth-generation Protestant, and the idea that I had been Catholic at one time was totally absurd. I had never been Catholic. I had never even been inside a Catholic church. My parents were both raised as Methodists, and my grandparents were church leaders. One of my great-grandfathers was a Methodist lay preacher. I never left the Catholic Church because I was never Catholic. The idea that I had intentionally decided to become Protestant was difficult to comprehend. Being Methodist was a natural thing for me, just as natural as another Mejicano being Catholic. I was born into a Protestant family and thus born into Protestantism.

We were also accused of turning our backs on our Mexican-American community and culture. Because we were not Catholic, we were not truly Mejicanos, people said. The prevalent idea at that time was that to be Mexican-American was to be Catholic. The Protestant faith was defined as the religion of Anglos. Thus, we were told that we were leaving the faith of our people and accepting the faith of the "gringo."

To suggest that we were not truly Mejicanos was unbelievable. We lived on La Calle Guadalupe in the barrio, attended Juan N. Seguin Elementary School, spoke Spanish as our first language, had *padrinos,* ate tortillas, *frijoles,* and *arroz,* and enjoyed our families like everyone else in the Seguin Mexican-American community. Our church was all-Mexican, and its program was conducted entirely in Spanish. The pastor, the church dignitaries, and the entire membership were Mejicanos from Seguin. I could not understand how we were any less *mejicano* than the rest and never did accept that notion.

Nonetheless, I realized that being Protestant meant certain things, which did not always enhance our social life in the Mejicano community. We did not drink beer, smoke, go to movies on Sunday, or go to dances. This does not mean that all Protestants abstained from such activities, but among the Protestants in our community that was the expectation. Thus many of us missed out on Saturday night dances, weekend movies, and socializing at the local bar. To this extent we did have the reputation of being *"santitos"* (little saints). Nothing was enjoyed more, or talked about more, among Catholics than when a Protestant was seen drinking or dancing. To this day, I claim that I do not know how to dance because I was raised a Protestant.

Unfortunately, many friendships were lost, romances truncated, and families split because of religion. Catholics would not date Protestants, and Protestant parents would advise their children to find Protestant partners. If a Catholic-Protestant couple became serious and marriage became a reality, one of them would have to leave their church. The priest would not marry a couple unless the

Protestant partner converted to Catholicism and agreed to rear the children in the Catholic Church. Because Protestants were in such a minority, Protestants left their Protestant churches much more often than Catholics left theirs to marry. In the event that a Protestant-Catholic couple did get married, which happened often, the consequences were usually painful. Families were split, married children became alienated from parents and siblings, and friendships ended. All of this occurred because of the religious divisions between *católicos* and *protestantes.*

To be fair, I also got an earful of criticism about Catholics from Protestants. I was taught that Catholics did not worship God but statues and idols, such as the Virgin Mary and the saints. Protestants considered this false worship and a sin. So whenever I walked by the Catholic church and peeked in, I could see what Protestants had been talking about. The crucifixes and statues depicting the suffering Christ were very frightening to me, as were the life-size statues of saints. I was also told that Catholics believed in a crucified and bleeding Christ but that we believed in a resurrected and living Christ. The Catholic Christ was sad, dead, or gory; our Protestant Christ was alive and looked happy. Ours was supposed to be a superior and more truthful understanding of Christ. In other words, I was taught that Protestants were right and Catholics were wrong.

Protestants would criticize Catholic practices such as praying the Rosary, maintaining home altars, confessing to a priest, and especially practicing acts of denial during Lent. Why, Protestants would ask, do you need beads to pray? Why pray to statues at home? Why confess to another human being? Why paint your forehead with ashes and do without certain desirable things during Lent but enjoy those things the rest of the year? How can Catholics understand the Mass when it is celebrated in Latin and not in Spanish? The Latin Mass was the basis for the Protestant claim that Catholics did not really understand their faith. There was considerable suspicion that Catholics did not study the Bible.

The severest criticism was reserved for homage and prayer to the Virgin Mary. Protestants did not believe that Mary had any special gifts or powers. She was another human being just like the rest of us. So why pray to her? Protestants were truly perplexed by the religious ways of their Catholic neighbors and saw much to find wrong and define as ignorant. There was a clear lesson for all Protestant children: our Protestant ways were not only superior to the Catholic ways, they were the true and enlightened ones.

The Catholic-Protestant division within the Hispanic community was a sad state of affairs. Religion was a subject you did not discuss with friends or relatives who were of the other religious tradition. In fact, many Catholic homes had signs on their doors stating that no Protestant propaganda would be accepted in that home: *"Este es un hogar católico. No se acepta propaganda protestante"* (This is a Catholic house. We do not accept Protestant propaganda). Catholics and Protestants did not visit each other's churches. People would not attend weddings, baptisms, or funerals because of these religious differences. Protestants could not be *padrinos* in Catholic baptisms, which meant that Catholics and Protestants could not be *compadres* or *comadres.* It was sad because the splits among friends, relatives, and neighbors brought pain and loss.

The Latino religious reality that I experienced as a child and as a young man in the Seguin of the 1940s and 1950s certainly reflected a pre-Vatican II mentality and dynamics. However, the Second Vatican Council, celebrated during the 1960s, brought many changes in the Catholic Church that improved the relationship with Protestant churches. One of the most visible was the introduction of the vernacular in the Mass and other church rituals. The use of Spanish opened the Mass to broader understanding by both Catholics and non-Catholics. Many Protestants began to see that the Mass had many similarities to the Protestant service of the Last Supper or Holy Communion. The Mass was Christian!

Another example of the changes brought by Vatican II was more frequent study of the Bible in Catholic circles. Protestants now found that they and their Catholic neighbors could discuss the Bible together. In addition, Catholic churches began to sing some of the same hymns and *coritos* that Protestants had sung for generations. In essence, the Second Vatican Council eliminated many barriers and made it possible for Hispanic Catholics and Protestants to share and to understand each other's traditions.

Protestants have also begun to change and be more receptive to Catholics. The ecumenical movement has influenced many Hispanic Protestants and created a broader sense of community among the various religious groups and traditions. Hispanic Protestants have become much more educated, knowledgeable, and appreciative about Catholics and other religious traditions and thus less judgmental toward others. The Protestant religious sector within the Hispanic community has itself become much more diverse. Diversity has forced many Protestants to be more accepting and open to other ways of knowing God.

Historically, the Chicano Movement also helped relations between Catholics and Protestants. It provided a shared vision and cause in the Mexican-American community. Catholics and Protestants shared a vision of social justice, and both affirmed that religious values were fundamental in the struggle against racism and discrimination. Protestants and Catholics joined hands in support of school walkouts, César Chávez, the grape boycott, voter registration, and many other community actions. Protestants and Catholics discovered that they were concerned about the same community and people, and thus they have become partners in many community concerns.

I have long since learned that both Catholics and Protestants need to take responsibility for the mutual intolerance and harsh attitudes of the past, and especially for teaching their children accordingly. I have also appreciated that many Catholics and Protestants have moved beyond such divisions and have sought each other out. Relations between Catholic priests and Protestant ministers have improved and flourished in many Hispanic communities. Joint weddings have been performed, and visits to each other's churches are more common. My sister Amelia began to play the organ at Our Lady of Guadalupe Church across the street from our home, and the local priest became a friend of the family. At the national level, Protestant and Catholic seminarians jointly participate in a united Hispanic Summer Program in theology. Many theological publications are inclusive of Catholic and Protestant perspectives. But much work needs to be done to improve relations between Catholics and Protestants so as to avoid the pain and divisions of the past.

Juan N. Seguin Elementary School

With the exception of Emma, all of our family began our educational journey at the same school that my father and mother attended. In fact, it was the school to which all Mejicanos were assigned. As early as I can recall, I wanted to go to school, and as a preschooler, I remember crying when my sisters left me behind as they went off to school. So it was an exciting time when it was my turn to go to school. The excitement began with the layaway shopping for school clothes; it continued through the pain of vaccinations and peaked with the morning preparation for my first day of school. I remember walking in a group that included my mother and sisters on the first day of school. All of us were filled with anticipation and excitement.

Mother taught me to respect my teacher and to respond to whatever the teacher asked of me by saying, "Yes, Ma'am." These were the only words of English that I knew as I set off for school. I felt quite confident; I knew some English. Little did I know that my limited knowledge of English would cause me trouble instead of making school easier for me. During those first days of school, the teacher began by teaching us some very basic English vocabulary. She would point to a picture of a dog, cat, or other figure and say the name out loud. For example, she might point to the picture of a dog and say, "This is a dog." She would then point to a student and ask, "What is this?" and the student was to respond by saying, "Dog." When my turn came, the teacher pointed to the picture and said, "This is a dog." I confidently said, "Yes, Ma'am." She was impressed with me. So she proceeded and instructed me, "Say dog." Again, I confidently responded with all due respect, "Yes, Ma'am." After repeating this scenario numerous times, my teacher, clearly very disappointed with me, instructed me to sit down.

The first year at elementary school was called preprimary. It was a year spent in language instruction and basic education, since most of us did not speak English and were not quite prepared to tackle first grade. As a result, most of us were already a year behind our Anglo and black counterparts. Eventually, those students who did well were allowed to "skip" a grade. I was one of those fortunate students, and I skipped the second grade. I lost my peers and attended school with children a year older and much bigger than I was. I enjoyed the honor, but I missed my cousins and friends.

Juan N. Seguin Elementary School was about seven blocks from our house. We walked to school in all kinds of weather. Mamadita's house was on our route, so it was a frequent stop after school. It was also a safe house in case we needed help. Walking to and from school was always an adventure. Living around the corner from Mamadita's house and on our route was an old African-American man who lived alone in a one-room shack. We all knew him as *el viejo de las papas* (the old potato man). Apparently he sold potatoes house to house in the barrio and usually carried a sack of potatoes over his shoulder. The frightening story told among schoolchildren was that, instead of potatoes, he had small children in that sack! We were scared to death of him and would always run at full speed past his house all the way to my great-grandmother's house. Needless to say, we never heard of anyone being caught and put in that sack.

Our school had no cafeteria or lunchroom. So all of us took our lunches. This usually consisted of a tortilla folded over with some refried beans and cheese tucked inside. Sometimes Mom would put an apple in our lunch sacks. And most of us children took our *taquito* lunches in paper sacks that had been used several times. To take white bread sandwiches for lunch was considered real status. The kids who took such lunches would proudly take their sandwiches out and eat them with gusto for the rest of us to see. Meanwhile, we would timidly pull the sacks up to our mouths and eat our tortillas hoping that no one could see what we were eating. There was one particular girl who earned the disdain of us all. She not only did not walk to school (her parents would drop her off each morning), but she even had an umbrella. But even more irritating was that she had a metal lunch box. And instead of tortilla *taquitos,* she always had white bread sandwiches. We called her *la roncha* (the sore), and no one would drink from the water fountain after she did; she was totally ostracized by the rest of us because of her car, her umbrella, her metal lunch box, and her sliced bread sandwiches.

As the school custodian, Papá Samuel helped make life easier for me. I got to see him every day, and the teachers knew he was my grandfather. I was free to run to his closet, leave things with him, or just visit. My grandfather was a special asset to me during marble season. The boys in school played marbles for keeps. There were two games we played. The first was *el posito,* or the little hole. We would dig a small hole in the ground, and one of two players would drop an even set of marbles into it. These represented an even contribution from two players. If an even number of marbles stayed in the hole, the player who dropped them in would win the marbles. If an odd number of marbles stayed in the hole, the second player would win. Our other game consisted of drawing a circle in the dirt, placing marbles in the center, and taking turns shooting them out. Some players were better than others, and some would lose many marbles. And some of the boys cried or complained to the teachers. So when the teachers saw a boy with a pocketful of marbles, the marbles were confiscated. This is where my grandfather came in. Whenever I won some marbles, I would take my winnings to him for safekeeping. He also gave me marbles that he had found on the school grounds. We had a good thing going for quite some time.

Attending Juan N. Seguin Elementary School was part of being Mexican-American in Seguin during my formative years. When my father attended the school, it was called Seguin Mexican School. It was our place. There was no choice. The school buildings themselves were the very same buildings in which my parents had studied. There was no cafeteria, gymnasium, or other amenities. The school building was situated next to a creek that flooded the barrio every time there was a significant rain. We accepted our assignment to Juan N. Seguin Elementary School as the proper thing for Mexican-Americans. It had been that way for generations. We accepted the facilities without question; we were grateful for what we had. Not surprisingly, many students dropped out early. Although I have many fond memories of friends and events from my school days, I am reminded that Juan N. Seguin Elementary School represented the historic practice of separation, segregation, and discrimination on the basis of ethnicity. The entire student body was Mexican-American. With one exception, all the teachers and administrators were Anglo. My grandfather, the janitor, was the only visible Mexican-American on the staff.

Seguin Schools in White, Black, and Brown

Before the 1960s the city of Seguin had a segregated school system. There was a distinct set of schools for blacks: an elementary school, a junior high school, and a high school. Ball High School, which blacks attended, was just across the gravel pit from our house and was a constant reminder to us of the system. Not that we needed such a reminder; we Hispanics also had our designated schools. However, ours was a modified system. Juan N. Seguin Elementary School was the only one open to Mexican-Americans regardless of where we lived in Seguin. For many years and for many Mexican-Americans, completing elementary school was a major accomplishment, and many children dropped out of school at that point. Those who made it into junior or senior high entered a very different school environment where the majority of the students were white. It was rare for a Mexican-American to graduate from high school. So we were very proud when our sister, Anita, was among the first Hispanics to graduate from Seguin High School.

Anglos attended several elementary schools in town, then went to Mary B. Erskine Junior High School and, of course, on to Seguin High School. The system was such that as Latinos, we were totally isolated from other racial or ethnic groups until we were in junior high, and then only those who continued beyond elementary school had that experience. Many Latinos never had an Anglo as a peer in school. I did not meet an Anglo my age until I entered junior high. Because blacks were still attending segregated schools, I never had a black classmate in the public schools of Seguin.

The junior high school we attended was not in the barrio; it was on the Anglo side of town. This meant we had to cross Guadalupe Street every day and enter a totally new world. We went from Juan N. Seguin Elementary School, where Hispanics were 100 percent of the school population to a new school in which we were a dramatic minority. It was a completely new culture, with a new set of rules, social reality, and pecking order. We Hispanics sought each other out for social and emotional support. It was obvious from the very beginning that we were competing with native English speakers, students with greater access to money, and students who had attended elementary schools with greater resources. While most of our classmates had parents who spoke English and had themselves spoken English all their lives, we were using a language foreign to our culture and upbringing. We became hesitant to use our English. We stopped speaking out in class and became the silent minority. We were poor and thrown into a social context in which the majority had better clothing, fancier school supplies, and money in their pockets for lunch. Sadly, many Mejicanos did not last long in this environment. It seems that the farther I progressed in school, the fewer Mexican-Americans there were.

By the end of my first year of junior high school, I had begun to make friends with some of the Anglo students and to participate in extracurricular activities. Because of the music interest in my family, I joined the band and played the cornet, as my sisters Anita and Licha had done before me. There were very few Hispanics in band, but we stayed with it throughout our public school careers. I also developed an interest in tennis and often played before and after school. I do not know how she managed financially, but my mother bought me a tennis racket, and I probably became the first kid in the barrio to play the game. There were no Mejicanos playing tennis, so I played with Anglo kids. This led to many friendships and to my school nickname, "Maldo."

I have often wondered how it was that my sisters and I managed to make it through the Seguin school system. We started out in elementary school in a completely segregated environment and then were thrust into an integrated and challenging environment in junior high. Neither of our parents had received a formal education; both had dropped out of school early on. No one in our extended family had graduated from high school, and most of our neighbors were in the same situation. I cannot help but believe we succeeded because of our parents' vision and commitment to work for the sake of the family. They devoted all their energy and resources to our well-being and education. Dad worked seven days a week and Mother worked six days a week outside the home so that we could have what we needed for school, even band instruments and a tennis racquet, not to mention a set of encyclopedias. But the church gave us self-respect and a sense of worth, social support, positive values, and leadership opportunities as youth that helped us to believe in ourselves. As the external environment challenged us because of our ethnicity, the family and church strengthened us internally to survive and to thrive.

The house on Guadalupe Street undergoing renovation. Shows the reuse of old lumber.

Dressed up for church. Mother with Anita, Rachel, Emma, Alejandro, and David.

The Maldonado siblings. Anita, Alicia, David, and Amelia in the back row; Rachel, Alejandro, and Emma in the front row.

Alejandro and David on el portal.

The author and his parents, David and Anita Maldonado, on the day he left Seguin.

Norberto Molina (Papagrande) with his Bible, ready for church on a Sunday morning.

The children of la iglesia metodista*; the author is in the front row wearing a striped shirt.*

Adults of the church. Papagrande at the far left in the back row; Mamagrande third from the left in the second row.

Samuel Maldonado (Papá Samuel) when he was custodian at Juan N. Seguin Elementary School.

Mamadita (Amada Gonzalez) seated and Mamagrande standing on her left.

At the old Seguin Mexican School that later became the Juan N. Seguin Elementary School.

Negros y Negritos

One of my regrets about my childhood days in Seguin is that I never had an African-American friend or peer. Seguin was racially and ethnically divided. One's race or ethnicity determined schools, neighborhoods, jobs, relationships, and everyday life. Hispanic children and many women could go through an entire day, week, or month without coming into contact with a person outside their ethnic group. Men and women who worked outside the home were more likely to interact with other ethnic groups, with Anglo bosses and with blacks as peers in the workplace.

Generations of suspicion and ignorance kept us apart and in constant fear of each other. Even the churches were segregated.

For example, there were three Methodist churches: a black Methodist church, La Trinidad Iglesia Metodista, and the white church, First Methodist. Likewise, there were three swimming pools in Seguin, one for each racial or ethnic population. Barbershops and restaurants were segregated. African-Americans even had their own funeral homes. As a result, my generation and those before me came out of a racially determined social reality that denied us the opportunity to know each other as peers.

Because of similarly poor socioeconomic conditions, Hispanics and blacks lived in the same sectors of Seguin, although there were distinct Mexican barrios and black neighborhoods. Many of these areas were adjacent to each other. As a result, there was a lot of visual contact but very little meaningful social contact or interaction between Mexican-Americans and African-Americans at that time. Language differences, ignorance, and mutual prejudices kept the Hispanic and black communities apart, and at times in tension or outright conflict. This was especially true among the youth. We had to use the same streets and thus crossed paths to go to different schools. Unfortunately, it was not unusual to engage in taunting, rock throwing, and fights. These outbreaks could not be settled in school because we were under separate administrators. Adults did not address these issues because they did not want to get involved, especially with the other group of whom they were ignorant and fearful. Nor did they know the parents, so there was no common forum.

Next to Ball High School was the public swimming pool for African-Americans. This meant that there was constant foot traffic past our house by black children going to school or to the swimming pool during the summer months. All of them were strangers and persons to avoid or ignore.

I recall one occasion when, somehow, my cousins arranged a baseball game between the barrio kids and the black kids. We played this game next door to Tía Chavela's house, so we felt safe. We must have played all day long; it was a unique, enjoyable day in a long tradition of racial and ethnic tensions in Seguin. We had discovered a common activity in which we all found pleasure and shared it for one day.

The general term that was applied to all black people was *negros*. However, children, the elderly, or those whom we knew were called *negritos,* a diminutive term that connotes familiarity, endearment, or lack of threat. Thus we referred to Mr. Jones who lived on Guadalupe Street as *"el negrito,"* but those whom we did not know were *"los negros."*

My father seemed to have a special relationship with older African-American men who walked by the house. He would sit out in the yard and greet them by tipping his hat, and they would respond with a similar gesture. He would also call out, "How do? Fine, thank you." The usual response was, "Fine, thank you." The exchange was smooth, cordial, and automatic. Watching my dad made me wonder how he was able to relate to African-Americans while I lived in constant tension with African-Americans my age. I have since realized that it was the larger context and racial system that kept us apart, made us fearful of each other, and never gave us the opportunity to be friends.

Meeting the Anglos

I did not have an Anglo peer or friend until I was twelve years old and in junior high school. My entire life had been spent in the barrio. My world had been *mi familia, la iglesia Metodista mejicana,* and Juan N. Seguin Elementary School. Anglos were totally unknown to me. Anglos lived in another part of Seguin, and that was another world. I read about them in textbooks. In fact, they were the only ones we read about in school. All the characters in our reading books were children with blond hair and blue eyes and had names like Dick and Jane, while all of us had dark hair and dark eyes and had names like Ricardo and Juanita. Also, the things Dick and Jane did in the textbooks were not the things we did on Guadalupe Street. So Anglos and their world were a mystery to me.

The Anglos I knew were the schoolteachers at elementary school and the police officers who occasionally drove through the barrio. In other words, the only Anglos I knew were adults in positions of authority. I had seen some of their cars and homes across Guadalupe Street, and they were incredibly beautiful in my eyes. I also knew that my mother would leave us to go clean Anglo families' houses, take care of their children, and do their wash. To a large extent, it was difficult to separate authority, power, and wealth from being Anglo. As a small child, I thought that to be Anglo was to be rich and powerful, and that this was the way the world was meant to be.

I also assumed that Anglos were the smart ones and that their language was superior. They were the teachers, police officers, and owners of big houses. They spoke as if they knew many things. They also spoke English, and so English must be the smart language. Our textbooks were in English, the television programs were in English, and the signs on store windows in town were in English. In school, we were taught not to speak Spanish, that English was better. Mexican-American children who learned English as their first language were considered the better students. They had to be more capable, and what they said must be true and the intelligent thing to say. Somehow, English and being intelligent were related. The Anglos were not only rich and powerful; they were also intelligent.

I finally got to see and meet Anglo children my own age when I entered Mary B. Erskine Junior High School. Entering that school was as frightening and anxiety-filled as the very first day of school at Juan N. Seguin Elementary School. I was scared and had no idea what to expect. Not only was Mary B. in an Anglo part of town, but the majority of children were Anglo; all of a sudden I was a minority again. Because many of my previous classmates had dropped out of school, we Mexican-Americans were a very small minority in junior high. In a classroom of approximately twenty-five students, there were four or five Hispanic students. And most of the teachers at Mary B. Erskine could not pronounce our Spanish names. They not only butchered our names when calling roll but also called them out in a questioning tone, which generated laughter among the other students; the teacher would quickly ask us to say our names out loud for them. Their usual response consisted of saying how pretty our Spanish names were, but they proceeded to give us English pronunciations of our names anyway. It was an early form of calling attention to our differences, and it would define us as different.

In elementary school I had been considered one of the more capable students. I had even skipped a grade and tutored other students. I had received special awards for my academic achievements. But I was now on the other side of Guadalupe Street at Mary B. Erskine Junior High School. All the Anglo students from Seguin and the surrounding rural areas attended this school. These were kids whose parents were teachers, professors at Texas Lutheran College, business owners, and owners of the big houses my mother cleaned. I was overwhelmed by the whole situation and by its newness, but most of all I was overwhelmed by the challenges of dealing with an Anglo world.

High school days were difficult also. First, there were even fewer Latinos. Our circle got smaller every year. Those of us who continued in school relied more and more on each other for mutual support. Hanging out together before school, during lunch, and after school was not for the purpose of separating ourselves; rather, we did it to find support and understanding of what we were all experiencing. Dating across ethnic lines was not an option. Anglos would not date Hispanics, and we did not even think of dating an Anglo. I remember that for the junior/senior prom, there were so few of us, especially boys, that we all agreed to attend the prom together without dates.

There were some exceptions. I developed a close friendship with Charles Branning. We were in the same grade, and we learned that both of us were Methodists, although he attended First Methodist and I attended La Trinidad. We joined forces and brought the youth groups of our churches together for many events. Charles and I also played tennis and enjoyed each other's friendship. Other Anglos also befriended me around the tennis courts and in the band.

I had to learn to live in two worlds—my world of La Calle Guadalupe, *mi familia,* and *la iglesia metodista* and the Anglo world across Guadalupe Street. I learned to live a major part of my daily life in an Anglo reality where I dealt with and competed with Anglos while trying to make sense of the entire situation. Going back and forth between La Calle Guadalupe and Mary B. Erskine Junior High School was a daily transition for me. It involved going from a world of Mamagrande, Mother's tortillas, Spanish, our barrio, the house on Guadalupe Street, and my extended family to a different world of Mrs. Waldrip, English, cafeteria meals, tennis courts, and school. I was "David" during the day and "Mijo" in the evening. If you were to survive and do well in school, you had to learn English, develop a thick skin about being Mexican-American, and learn to compete with Anglo kids.

While a handful of Mexican-American boys chose to play team sports and found a niche in school life, I chose academics, band, and tennis. These were not macho activities. Nonetheless, they were areas that served me well in finding my place and in getting to know Anglos as peers. I was fortunate to do well in my classes. Being on the honor roll did not hurt in getting the teachers' attention and in earning some respect from other students.

Playing in the band was both a treat and a burden. I enjoyed music and the personal satisfaction of playing the cornet. I was also impressed at how good we sounded together. Being part of a group effort gave me a sense of belonging. Marching in unison and playing in a concert taught me that the rest of the group depended on my doing well. Participating in the band also facilitated many friendships. Rehearsals, parades, trips, football games, and concerts—all of this brought me closer to Anglos than I ever expected. The burden for me was attending practices after school, carrying my instrument case through the barrio, and having to wear the military-style uniforms.

But at the end of the day I still went home across Guadalupe Street to *mi familia.* And the Anglo students went home to their neighborhoods. We went our separate ways. So for me interaction with Anglos was limited to the school grounds and band activities. There was no social interaction between the two cultural groups in our neighborhoods or homes. I did not visit in their homes, nor did they come to mine. And certainly, there was no such thing as spending the night at each other's homes. This was just the way it was. At the end of the school day you were still a Mexican-American and you went to your own neighborhood.

Going home meant going back to my barrio street and our way of life as it was before I had ventured out into the Anglo world of junior high school. It meant returning to my house, family, barrio, and extended family. In a way, it was a daily return to the safety and warmth of a world in which you were not competing or being negatively defined, where you could speak the language of your *abuelitos* and simply be yourself. This was a daily transition and retreat, which provided safety, acceptance, and the warmth of family. The next day it started all over again.

The daily return to the barrio and your own home also meant dealing with all its realities. It meant sleeping several children to a bed, cramped study space, and accepting the fact that your family did not have money for many of the things you wanted or sometimes needed.

The daily transition between an Anglo world and our barrio home was made easier by my three older sisters, who continued in school until they graduated. This helped me to realize that graduating from high school was possible and that I could do it too. It was also made easier by my parents, who provided incredible emotional support and worked long hours to provide for our needs. Junior and senior high school were challenging years for us. Yet they were very satisfying ones: we were able to accomplish things that our parents could only dream of. We accomplished their dreams. They also lived in two worlds, but their lives in the Anglo world were ones of subordination. We learned to live in two worlds in a new and challenging way. We crossed Guadalupe Street every day.

Being Mexican-American

As a small child, my world was homogeneous. I felt safe and secure in it. My Mexican-American world of extended family, barrio, and church was predictable and accepting. They gave me a sense of belonging. Yet when I crossed Guadalupe Street and entered the Anglo world, I confronted a reality that was as new as it was powerful, initially confusing, and at times frustrating. Contact with Anglos made me aware that I was Mexican-American and thus different.

In the barrio and within the family, we referred to ourselves as Mexican or Mejicanos. To be Mexican meant to have Mexican ancestry and to look Mexican. Barrio people referred to "having Mexican blood" and to "looking Mexican"; this was essentially a racial definition. We were a race (*una raza*), a people who shared certain physical characteristics. Likewise, to be Mexican was to speak Spanish and to engage in Mexican activities. To be Mexican was to enjoy our common language, music, foods, social events, family systems, and identity. This was a cultural definition. We were comfortable with and proud of our self-definitions of being Mexican. Our Mexican ancestry and culture were things we considered natural and good. We enjoyed being Mexican. Ethnicity was not a point of contention, nor was it much discussed. It was just the way our world was. For a small child, race and culture were things you did not ask about, much less define or compare.

Contact with the Anglo world gave being Mexican a new and different meaning; to be Mexican was to be different, especially from the Anglo point of view, or at least that is how we perceived it. It meant we were *not* Anglo. The newness of the definition came in the first experiences of being called a Mexican by Anglos. This happened when I entered the Anglo world for the first time in junior high school. There, I experienced the definition of "Mexican" in a way different from the way we defined Mexican and used the term in the barrio. In the barrio, being "Mexican" meant that you belonged; in the Anglo world, it meant that you did not belong, that you were a foreigner and an outsider.

Entering the Anglo world also exposed me to the confusing notion that we were from Mexico. How could we be from Mexico, if we were born and lived all our lives in Seguin? I remember Anglo children asking me when my family and I came from Mexico. Or they wanted to know from which part of Mexico I had come. This was frustrating, confusing, and eventually annoying to me. Even after having asserted my Seguin roots, I was still considered a Mexican. It was a powerful definition of exclusion.

But among Mexican-Americans, to be a Mexican in those days did not involve any question of national loyalty. We knew ourselves to be American citizens. Mexican-American families took great pride in serving in the military. From the Maldonado family, Uncle Sammy volunteered to serve in the naval air force and

Tío Berna served in the navy during World War II. On my mother's side, a cousin was killed in the European battles. To see a Mexican-American soldier in uniform was a source of pride for the entire barrio. So the notion that we were foreigners and not fully American was confusing and insulting.

To be defined as Mexican also meant racial distinction among Anglos. Although in the barrio we used the term "Mexican" to define ourselves as a people with a distinct ancestry, it did not carry the connotation of inferiority. In the Anglo world, to be non-Anglo was to be inferior. This carried distinct social consequences. Social separation was considered important and served as a powerful tool. Dating across these two groups was socially frowned on, and marriages between Anglos and Mexican-Americans were especially to be avoided. In school, ethnic cliques were the norm.

Ethnic and racial definitions were powerful social constructs. They defined us and determined where we lived, where we went to school, who our friends would be, and the lives of most people from the barrio. It was not something you could outgrow, overcome through study or wages or escape, even if you wanted to. It was a powerful reality in Seguin, in Texas, and in the United States.

So I was a Mexican boy from Guadalupe Street in Seguin. I learned that my family, church, and neighborhood and I were different from the Anglo world and from the African-American world. Although my parents, grandparents, and great-grandparents had long and deep roots in Texas, dating back to the 1850s, and the closest association with Mexico was that it was the birthplace of two great-grandparents, I was still a Mexican. I was a Mexican-American.

Piscando Algodón and Books

Picking cotton, or, as we say, *piscando algodón, el algodón,* or *las piscas,* is one of those experiences that many Mexican-Americans in Texas shared. Entire families loaded up their straw sombreros, babies, and belongings on the back of a truck and headed *al norte para las piscas* (north to picking). Many families went far north beyond Texas to work the crops, including *el vetabel* (sugar beets), *la papa* (potatoes), and *la cheri* (cherries). Families who migrated beyond Texas left in the spring and returned home in the fall. You could always tell when it was time for the annual trek to crops in the north, because children would begin to leave school before the end of the academic year; these students usually returned after school had started in the fall.

You could also see their homes boarded up through the summer months.

Every spring *troqueros* (truckers) combed the neighborhoods and family networks recruiting "hands" for the season. I always had a problem with calling workers "hands." It sounded like we were defined simply as instruments of labor; there was more to us than just our hands. We had minds, spirits, and hearts. We also had stomachs. But in the springtime, we were "hands" and that was what the *troqueros* wanted. They had already been up north and had contracted with farmers there for a certain number of workers. I doubt that they discussed or negotiated beyond what our hands could do.

The *troqueros* always painted a rosy picture for the recruits. *El norte* held many dreams. Families were promised that they could make lots of money, especially if the children also worked. If you were over ten years old, you were considered a "hand." This meant you could pull a cotton sack and bring in money for the family, and also for the *troquero. Troqueros* made agreements with farmers for hands in exchange for a cut for himself, a certain price per pound, and housing for the workers. Housing was a critical matter. Farmers owned the land and the crops and controlled the housing. If you worked for a certain farmer, you worked on his terms or you were without a job and on the streets with no housing. *Troqueros* played a crucial and powerful role. You had to go through a *troquero* to get work. If you had problems with the *troquero,* you and your family were out of a job and a house.

Every spring *troqueros* could be seen in Seguin picking up families and delivering them to specific farmers all over Texas or farther up north. One summer, the promise of money to be made was just too much for us. Besides, Mamagrande needed to get away after the death of Papagrande. We were a large family of seven children who needed the income and had the potential to bring in a relatively significant amount of additional money. Since our father had a steady job at the golf course, he wisely chose not to leave it. The rest of us were loaded into the back of a truck one early summer morning, and along with my mother and Mamagrande, we went off to pick cotton. We had waited until school was out; in retrospect, I think I know why.

The *troquero* who recruited my family was the common-law husband of a maternal great-aunt. We knew him as José. We never called him Tío, though we did call our great-aunt Tía Goya. José had two sons from a previous marriage, Valentine and Gilberto, who were in their late teens and had the reputation of being top-of-the-line cotton pickers. José could also hold his own picking cotton. His family went to pick cotton every year; compared to them we were rookies in the cotton fields.

It was before dawn when we set out. Seguin was dark; even the dogs were asleep. Most of the children were half asleep, yet excited about this new adventure. We had never picked cotton before and had never spent a night away from home or Seguin. Now we were driving more than one hundred miles from Seguin to pick cotton in East Texas. Just sitting in the back of a large truck with our mother and grandmother was something to remember. Mother had packed lunch, which consisted of the usual *taquitos* of flour tortillas, beans, and cheese. We had our hats, jeans, and work shirts; we were ready to pick cotton, although we had never seen a cotton plant in our entire lives.

We arrived at what must have been the most remote rural area in southeastern Texas. There were no buildings, parks, stores, or schools to be seen for miles. I was convinced that we were lost in the middle of nowhere. But there in the middle of nowhere was a house. Actually, it was a shack that was to be our home for the rest of the summer. The walls were unpainted, and it had no fans; the floors were wooden and splintery. But the shack did have a big covered porch. It must have had a couple of rooms besides the kitchen. The children, our mother, and our grandmother slept on the floor; some of the married adults slept in the other rooms; and many other adults slept outside, on the porch or on cots under the trees.

It was incredible how quickly things became organized as soon as we arrived. Mamagrande stayed at the house with the youngest children, my brother Cando and sister Emma, who were not old enough to work in the fields. Mamagrande prepared the noon meal and watched over the youngsters. The rest of us left at daybreak to *piscar algodón*. Our attire consisted of jeans, long-sleeved shirts to protect us from the sun, and straw hats. A popular thing to do when it got really hot was to wet the hat and put it back on while it was still wet. Picking cotton was a simple but painstaking task. We were given a long sack with a strap that fit around our neck and shoulders; the older you were, the longer the sack and thus the more cotton you could pick. Each one of us was given a particular row to pick. This was exciting at the beginning. But it did not take long to realize that it was backbreaking work. Our task was to fill our sacks with cotton and bring them in to be weighed.

Usually, there was a large truck or trailer onto which the cotton was unloaded; a weighing machine hung at one corner of the truck. One person, usually the *troquero* or some other reliable individual, was given the task of weighing the sacks of cotton, recording the weight, and emptying the cotton onto the truck. The weigh-ins were always special moments in the day. Workers who were close by would gather around to see how much a particular individual had picked. There were personal records, family records, daily records, and group records. There was special status accorded anyone who held a weight record. I don't think I ever held such a status other than my own personal weight record.

Coming in to weigh was always a time for a much-needed and much-desired quick break. We would gulp the ice water, wet our hats and bandannas, shake the dirt out of our shoes, and head back out to our designated rows after the weigh-ins. Lunchtime was also a special time. Mamagrande would have prepared *taquitos de frijoles*, cheese, and sometimes baloney. We loved to sit in the shade of the trailer and on top of the partially filled sacks; we made sure that there was still some cotton in them; they made great pillows. Talk around lunchtime was about the heat, the number of pounds picked, records set that morning, and what we planned to do on Saturday.

After picking cotton all week, Saturday was a welcome relief. It meant payday. This was the day when we would all bathe and get to wear the best clothes we had brought, which usually meant clean jeans. We would all jump onto the truck and head into town. For the adults, it meant buying groceries for the following week; for us kids, it meant buying the biggest and coldest soda water (soft drink) we could find. We did not go to movies or dances. It was strictly a day spent shopping for food and maybe a visit to the dime store. We were usually home by late afternoon and spent the rest of the day just playing and relaxing under the trees.

Sunday was still another day of rest, but it was also a day for church. My great-aunt and her *troquero* husband were Pentecostal, so we usually participated in Pentecostal services. This was certainly not like church in Seguin at La Trinidad Iglesia Metodista. Here, we had church services outside under the trees. People offered *testimonios* and sang *coritos,* and there was much hand clapping. I was amazed that the congregation clapped their hands during the religious service. I had been taught to be respectful of the church sanctuary, especially during *servicios*. In Seguin we were not allowed to make noise in church. But here the Pentecostals were making all sorts of noise, and the ones making the noise were the adults. They seemed so happy and to really enjoy church. They had smiles on their faces, movement in their bodies, and thunder in their hands. You can well imagine the reaction we got when we returned to Seguin and told our minister about the Pentecostal services.

Picking cotton that summer was a special experience for me and, I am sure, for the rest of my family. I have many vivid memories of those weeks in the cotton fields, but the most impressive was what happened when we returned to Seguin. The entire family had worked in the fields and made some money. Mother was the head of the family on this adventure, and she saved every penny we made. We thought the money would be used for back-to-school clothing and other necessities. We all knew that the house needed repairs. And our parents had other bills that needed to be paid as well. There were many things on which our mother could have spent the money. But she did something we did not expect. She bought the family a set of the World Book Encyclopedia.

Buying the encyclopedias was probably one of the most powerful examples our mother could have given us. This purchase, with savings from picking cotton, opened our eyes to the world of books, words, and learning. I still remember the day the encyclopedias arrived and the excitement we all felt as we opened each book. We yelled out all the subjects we found. "*¡Mira!* Look at this! Wow, look at this picture of a snake!" We were overwhelmed and impressed. Those encyclopedias became a daily source of learning, entertainment, help with homework and reports, and just plain reading. My mother was responsible for this. Somehow she had this dream that her family ought to have encyclopedias. We picked cotton all summer and dreamed of many things. But we never dreamed of a set of encyclopedias. Mother did, and we are richer because of her vision.

El Diez y Seis de Septiembre

There was one day of the year when we could celebrate being Mexican in Seguin. That was *El Diez y Seis de Septiembre* (September 16), Mexican Independence Day. I connected it with Mexico only vaguely. In fact, we did not have Mexico in mind when we "made fiesta"; we were simply celebrating being ourselves. The Mexican-Americans of Seguin all came together to celebrate and enjoy our music, food, colors, and each other. It was not political; it was a cultural and community event.

El Diez y Seis was actually more than just one day; it involved several days of *fiestas patrias* at La Plataforma Hidalgo, an open-air dance floor consisting of a concrete slab in the midst of a dusty or muddy field (depending on the weather) on the edge of town and in El Barrio Apache. It might be flooded several times a year, but it always served as the central focus for Mexican dances and fiestas. And on El Diez y Seis de Septiembre, that was the place to be, and almost every Mexican-American in Seguin was sure to be there.

Hundreds of people congregated every year to enjoy the carnival, dancing, eating, and visiting with friends and *compadres;* and for the youth of the community, walking flirtatiously around the *puestos* (booths) was the order of the day and evening. Dances were held in the evenings and featured live bands playing Mexican polkas and *norteñas.* Sampling of the many savory dishes went on throughout the day and into the night. The women provided a sumptuous variety of *comidas mejicanas* in the many *puestos* surrounding the dance area. There were *tamales, tacos, bunuelos, enchiladas*, and of course *frijoles y arroz*. For dessert or simply to cool off, you could crunch on *raspas* that came in a variety of flavors. We crunched snowcones until they dripped all over our hands. There were huge bottles of Big Red, Dr. Pepper, and root beer for quenching our parched throats. And beer. There was always plenty of beer and people willing to drink too much. These celebrants were usually taken away by friends or the ever-present *policía.*

The Diez y Seis de Septiembre that I remember most vividly was when Anita, my oldest sister, was crowned *Reina del Diez y Seis de Septiembre* (Queen of September 16 Fiestas). This was quite an honor that included having her picture in the Seguin newspapers and on the cover of the Fiesta Program, as well as marching out onto the center of the dance floor escorted by a handsome young man and followed by her royal court. She was treated royally and received much publicity in Seguin and especially among the Mexican-American community. How was she chosen? By the simple process of selling votes. Apparently, every contestant was to sell votes at one penny each during a certain period. The one who sold the most votes would be crowned Queen. Anita and her friends, including our family, sold the most tickets for her candidacy that year, and so she received the crown. Needless to say, we were very proud and happy for her. She was a beautiful queen and enjoyed every second of her reign.

Unfortunately, Anita's participation in the fiestas did not sit well with the minister of our church. He was a conservative man and believed that dancing or simply being where dancing was going on and where beer was served was a sin. It was not a place for good church people. He gave our parents a hard time over the matter. Nonetheless, Anita was queen and we celebrated.

Gente del Pueblo

Seguin had many characters. Although they might have been institutionalized in some towns, in Seguin they were part of the community, and people just looked after them. Tento, who lived in one of Mamadita's houses, was one such character. He had Down Syndrome. He was a gentle soul with a permanent smile on his face. Tento wore denim overalls, tennis shoes, and a cap, usually with the brim turned up. He was a downtown presence, sweeping sidewalks and running errands for a handout. No one took advantage of him; instead, Seguin folks took care of him.

And there was Chevo. He walked the town day and night, main and side streets, downtown and in the neighborhoods. He smiled at everyone, yet was always alone. You found him at the swimming pool and the drugstore. He was everywhere. And Chevo probably attended every church in Seguin.

When he attended our church, Chevo sat right up in front, in a very prominent place. He marched up the aisle and took his seat with confidence and assurance. After the recessional, he participated enthusiastically in the greetings among the congregation, and he attended every church social event. He appeared in more wedding pictures, as a member of the congregation, than people cared to count. Seguin also provided a place for Chevo.

Watching Tento and Chevo on the streets of Seguin taught me a great deal about how a community not just tolerates, but actually respects and cares for those who cannot care for themselves. There were some who made fun of their peculiar ways, but Tento and Chevo helped to make Seguin a special place.

As a small child, I lived in the protective embrace of my extended family and was not exposed to many characters beyond *la familia*. But there was one that we could not avoid and from whom I could not be shielded. He was Don Adolfo, our neighbor. He was the patriarch of the Rodríquez clan who lived next door to us and who, like the Molinas and Maldonados, also had an extensive extended family living in a cluster of houses on his lot. There were at least three households next door to us representing the same generational distribution as our extended family. Each generation had its battles with the neighbors. The children fought with the neighbor children, the adults did battle with the neighboring adults, and the patriarchs had their run-ins with their own counterparts. It was a classic case of contending neighbors.

I do not know how or when the dispute began, but I believe it was probably a matter of territory. It probably started between Papagrande and Don Adolfo when my grandfather and father bought and built on our lot, which had been vacant up to that point. My grandfather and father believed in fences, and they built one where one had not existed before between our property and Don Adolfo's. We also claimed our part of the gravel pit as our property. It seems that Don Adolfo had been using the gravel pit as a grazing area for his cows and goats. With the fences and claims of the newcomers, the Maldonados and Molinas, Don Adolfo was not only fenced in but also lost the use of that land. Thus the battle began and continued at every opportunity.

Don Adolfo would get into verbal exchanges with Papagrande, cut across our land, and generally make a nuisance of himself. As small children, we always avoided Don Adolfo when he was outside, in the gravel pit, or walking across the front of our property. He was a grumpy fellow who seemed always to be in a bad mood. One time he even stopped a funeral procession in front of his house to ask who had died. The last I remember of him was when he was on his deathbed. You could hear his loud cries as he screamed for his wife to hold him. I mention Don Adolfo as a character in Seguin because he was one of the first persons I recall outside my extended family. He made our lives a daily challenge and brought some degree of fear, all because of fences between neighbors.

Most of the people I knew as a child were barrio people or members of the church; as a teenager, I met many more people when I worked in a department store. Among the many people I knew by the time I left Seguin, I have a special memory of and respect for Isaac Garza. Isaac was a short man, not over five feet tall. I knew him as one who always walked to church. He did not have a car until late in life (after I left Seguin). He was always well dressed, although his clothes were usually too long for him, but he wore them with pride and dignity. His ties reached well below his belt or were tucked into his pants. He wore stays to hold up the long shirtsleeves, and his hands would disappear into the sleeves of his coat. He always wore a hat, tilted to the side, and he had a full mustache. His height might have presented a challenge to him in finding clothes that fit, but Isaac always dressed in a manner that showed self-respect.

Although he was a small man, Isaac was a giant in my book. He was the first Hispanic to work in the Guadalupe County Courthouse. The county courthouse sat right in the middle of town and served as a formidable institution and symbol. It represented the power of the Anglo establishment and housed all the county offices, including the justice of the peace, the county sheriff, and the county jail on the top floor. All were important offices for los Mejicanos de Seguin. The justice of the peace performed many of our shotgun weddings (other weddings took place in church), the sheriff arrested our friends, and the county jail housed some of our relatives. For generations, Latinos went to the courthouse either as consumers or visitors to the top floor—the county jail. No one from the Hispanic community went there to work, not until Isaac Garza!

Isaac Garza became the first Mexican-American who went to the courthouse to earn a living. He was the first Hispanic to have a key to the county courthouse. What was his job? He was the custodian. This may seem like a small accomplishment and nothing much to celebrate, but for us, Isaac Garza broke a barrier. He became a big man.

Another person who helped to shape the Seguin I knew was Cesario Guadarrama. We all knew him as "El Apache," or simply as Guadarrama; in church, he was Hermano (Brother) Guadarrama. I had the opportunity to know him better because he was a member of our church. But he played the kind of role in Seguin that made him known to every Latino in town, and so I probably would have known him anyway. He was the local *patrón,* the successful Hispanic businessman who had a hand in everything in the barrio for many years. The name "El Apache" came from his famous Mexican general store in the center of the barrio; this store was later converted to the Apache Mexican Restaurant. *La tienda* Apache was the mainstay of his early business ventures. He later developed a contracting business, a real estate company, and a barrio named for him, El Barrio Apache.

El Apache became widely known through his radio program, which was aired each day for a couple of hours in the early afternoon. It was the only local Spanish programming available to us. El Apache played songs, read the news, and plugged his big store and real estate business. He even had my three older sisters sing on the radio. His favorite ad was *"Cuando el Apache vende, la gente compra, desde un alfiler hasta una casa"* (When El Apache sells, the people buy, from a straight pin to a house). He tried to sell my father a house once, I saw him in action, but my father was too cautious and did not buy.

El Hermano Guadarrama taught the adult Sunday school class at our church for years. He always sat in the same spot every Sunday morning and probably was the biggest financial contributor to the church. He gave special attention and encouragement to young people and handed out bags of goodies to the children every Christmas Eve. As a leader of the church, he held every conceivable office at one time or another and contributed a beautiful stained glass window for the sanctuary. He was a classy fellow, well traveled, and one who handled his wealth with care. Why do I mention him as a memorable person from my Seguin past? I saw in him a sophisticated, self-educated person who learned to integrate his ethnicity and religious identity. He was a successful businessman and churchman, yet he was a Mexican-American who knew the barrio and served it well.

There were many other characters in Seguin whose names I cannot remember and with whom I never spoke. There was *"La Polviada"* (the powdered woman) who always carried a powder puff in her hands and wore heavy makeup as she walked through the barrio. There was "El Shorty" who lived across the gravel pit from us and spent most of his time drunk or *crudo* (hung over), beating up his wife, in jail, or riding his bicycle down the street at all hours of the day or night, whistling a song. And there was Vidal, whom all the girls feared because of his big face, loud voice, funny walk, and overly friendly behavior with young girls.

But the Seguin I knew was mainly a town of plain folks who worked hard for a living. They were unskilled or semiskilled blue-collar workers who used their hands and backs, usually outdoors in the heat or the cold. They received weekly paychecks that were cashed at the local grocery store. Many of them walked to town on Saturdays and to their churches on Sundays. Most were law-abiding citizens who worked hard to take care of their families. That is the Seguin I remember and the one that shaped who I am.

Seguin Leader Department Store

During the 1940s and 1950s, Seguin had a vibrant central business district, *el centro* (the center or downtown), which was built around the county courthouse. The business district served as the banking and commercial center for the county and was also the social crossroads for Seguin. Everybody in Seguin and Guadalupe County came downtown sooner or later. They came during the week to do business in the courthouse, such as posting bail, applying for marriage licenses, or taking care of other legal matters. All of the banks, dime stores, department stores, and drugstores were there, as was the only newsstand. Downtown Seguin was the crossroads for German farmers, Mexican-Americans, African-Americans, teenagers, retirees, the poor, the middle class, and the few wealthy persons in town. It was the place to be on Saturdays. People parked their pickup trucks or cars and visited from the parked vehicles. They strolled the several blocks of downtown and stopped to visit with passersby. Retired men had their special place—the bench at the corner of Austin and Court streets. This is where Papá Samuel sat right in the middle of town on the courthouse corner and greeted everyone walking by. We all crossed paths in *el centro*. If you stood on a downtown corner, sooner or later you saw practically everyone in Seguin.

Downtown Seguin was also the place for shopping, and the Seguin Leader Department Store was the most centrally located store. It was at the corner of Austin and Court streets, across from the courthouse. From its door, you could see up and down Austin—the main street in Seguin—and also up and down Court, the cross street. There was no better location in Seguin to see and to be seen. At the age of sixteen I got a job working in this store; the job lasted through high school.

My mother had worked at Seguin Leader Department Store for several years before I got a job there. She started as the seamstress who did all the alterations for the store but soon was in demand as a sales clerk. It was through her that I got the job. I used to go by the store to visit with her and got to know the manager and other workers there. The manager asked her if I would be interested in a job. Of course, I was. So in the summer of my sophomore year I started working six days a week. I earned a grand total of $18 per week working from 8:00 A.M. until 6:00 P.M. This amounted to $3 per day working full time. I thought I was rich! During the school year, I worked after school and on Saturdays, and earned even less. We were paid in cash in small brown envelopes every Monday after work. Mondays were good days.

My first duties included sweeping the sidewalks and the entire store every morning. Sweeping the sidewalk was a very public activity. Everyone passing by saw me and I saw them. I still remember how proud I felt going out with a broom to sweep the sidewalk. I used to take my time because I enjoyed being part of the morning ritual in downtown Seguin. You could wave to the other sweepers and to people going to work. I had a job at the Seguin Leader Department Store!

My indoor duties included sweeping the floors, receiving stock, and pricing and stocking merchandise. The job gave me responsibilities, experience, and exposure to dealing with people. I never dreamed of having a job at that age in Seguin. I went from playing ball in the gravel pit on La Calle Guadalupe to working in an air-conditioned store downtown. I even got to wear a dress shirt and tie on Saturdays.

My duties expanded to working on the sales floor. This was a quite a step for me. I had to learn to say, "May I help you?"—"*¿En que le puedo ayudar?*"—to people I had never spoken to before in my life. I had to take the initiative and approach people who were older. I helped old men buy overalls, men get their work shoes, cowboys fit into their boots, and teenagers buy their Levis, and I was only sixteen years old. It was a fantastic feeling to make a sale, to take a stack of merchandise up to the counter, and to write out a purchase receipt.

At that time there were three languages spoken in Seguin—English, Spanish, and German—and at Seguin Leader Department Store, we had sales staff who spoke all those languages. In the men's department, Alfredo Molina and I spoke Spanish and English; Mr. Reimer spoke German, English, and some Spanish. So when the old German farmers came in and asked in German, *"Sprechen Sie Deutsch?"* (Do you speak German?), I automatically pointed to Mr. Reimer. It got to the point that we knew most of the customers, including the good, the bad, and the ugly. There were customers from whom Alfredo and Mr. Reimer would hide because they did not want to wait on them, and so they were left to me. I was not on commission, so I also took the customers who were "just looking" or were the "come back Saturday" type.

Seguin Leader Department Store was also my first opportunity to know and work with Jews. I had never known any before. The only thing I knew about Jews was what I had heard in church, which was not too favorable, or what I had read in the Bible. Two Jewish brothers from San Antonio owned the store, and the store managers were also Jewish. What a relief and great surprise was in store for me. Jews turned out to be good people. In fact, they took me in and treated me with great sensitivity and kindness. One of them, Ralph, would talk to me about college, music, books, and the proper way men dressed. He showed me his car and once helped me paint the fog lights on our car. He was a good friend, and I recall him with appreciation. I was impressed by how these Jews treated a Mexican kid from Guadalupe Street. They helped me as I developed into a young man in Seguin.

Working at Seguin Leader Department Store downtown was an important introduction to diversity and provided me with the opportunity to relate to the various ethnic and cultural groups in the area. In addition to Anglos, I was introduced to Germans, African-Americans, and Jews. I also met many other Mexican-Americans I had seen only in the barrio. I met all these people as customers, work peers, and managers. As a sales clerk, I met people in a professional relationship and gained self-confidence. I also learned the value of being bilingual and learned to relate cross-culturally. Seguin Leader Department Store no longer exists, but in my mind and memory it stands as a major part of my development and my Seguin experience.

Leaving Seguin

Seguin's location close to San Antonio was a mixed blessing Only thirty miles separate the Guadalupe County Courthouse in the center of Seguin and the Alamo in downtown San Antonio. "San Anto" represented opportunity for the young and instilled fear in the hearts of adults in Seguin. The young saw San Antonio as the escape from the confines of a small town where everybody knew you and saw your every move. The adults saw San Antonio as the center of all the evils of the modern era. Every night on the news, first on the radio and later on television, we learned with horror about the accidents, murders, and sins of the city. As a result, whenever we drove in to San Antonio my father insisted on closing the car windows, even though we had no air-conditioning.

It is not surprising that the young left Seguin for the excitement and promises of San Antonio, Austin, or Houston. Seguin was a place to leave, especially if you were Chicano or dreamed about an education. The only college in town was Texas Lutheran, but it was private and very expensive. Many Mexican-Americans ended up working in *el pollo* (the poultry processing plant in town), doing manual labor for the city or the gas company, or being a yardman. If they were lucky and had connections, they worked at *el fierro* (the steel mill), which offered the best-paying jobs in the county; the cleanest jobs were those in the drugstores and the various department and grocery stores in town.

Leaving Seguin was a painful yet promising necessity for many young Mexican-Americans. They left Seguin for better jobs, an education, or simply to get away. For jobs, they went to San Antonio or Houston; for an education, they moved to Austin or San Marcos, which were only twenty-two miles away but far enough to be gone and out of Seguin. Joining the navy or the air force was also a popular means of getting away. I recall one of the Benavídez boys dropping out of the tenth grade to join the military. He wrote letters to our teacher, who would read them to us. We thought he was so lucky to be in distant and exotic places like California. Some people left to work in the agricultural fields up in *el norte* and never returned. I recall when my oldest sister, Anita, left home for San Antonio to attend business college. We all cried. It was like losing her to the big city, and we feared that we would never see her again. Many left Seguin never to return or be seen again. Anita never returned to live in Seguin again.

Leaving Seguin was also a social escape. To be in Seguin was to live in a place where your social position, opportunities, and economic access were determined by your race and ethnicity. Seguin, like many other small towns in Texas, consisted of three distinct realities—white, black, and brown. Each ethnic and racial group had its own schools, swimming pools, neighborhoods, jobs, and social roles. It was important to learn your place and the rules, if you were to survive and get along. As a Mexican in a town owned and controlled by Anglos, you learned to live with and in marginality. You knew the barbershops, restaurants, and places that served Mexicans; you also learned where not to go. Some places you would not even think of entering. Such a life was oppressive to anyone with dreams. To be free from such a segregated social environment meant leaving Seguin, the small town, and heading to the anonymity, diversity, and opportunities of the big cities.

It is a sad reality that so many young Chicanos had to leave Seguin to seek their dreams elsewhere. It is unfortunate that most did not return for the very same reasons. Yet we are all from Seguin, and Seguin made a lasting impression on all of us. I sometimes wonder if growing up in such a setting gave many young Mexican-Americans the desire for a better life elsewhere.

Nonetheless, there are those who never left Seguin and made it their lifelong home. Some became the core of the church and community leaders. They raised their families in Seguin and will probably be buried in Seguin. Many hold jobs in Seguin, but some commute to work in San Antonio or at Randolph Air Force Base nearby. Others traveled the world, especially in the military, and returned to Seguin to raise their families and continue their lives. These people have proven that you do not have to leave Seguin to find happiness and comfort. They found both right at home in Seguin. Sometimes I envy these natives who have stayed in Seguin. But I was one of those who left. Yet when I return I am one of them. I am from Seguin.

Visiting Seguin

Every time I return to Seguin, which is usually to visit my mother or attend a family funeral, I enter a place of memories. My mind and Seguin seem to play games with each other. Seguin does not seem to have changed much since I left almost forty years ago, or is it that I do not let it change in my mind? What I see is exactly what I remember, and what I remember is confirmed by what I see. Changes are explained away as progress; sometimes they are defined as intrusions. Seguin is a particular time and place from 1943 to 1960 experienced by a Mexican-American kid.

I usually enter Seguin from the north on Highway 123. The old 123 used to go right through downtown as Austin Street, and everyone going to the Gulf Coast went through "downtown."

Today, there is an efficient bypass that denies travelers the pleasure of seeing Seguin. Today, they miss the big pecan, the Guadalupe County Courthouse, and the bench where my grandfather used to sit every day with his friends. They also do not see the plaza, with its splashing fountain, that used to be the center of town; the Texas Theater, where I watched Cantinflas movies; and Max Starke Park, where my father mowed golf greens for thirty years.

Old Highway 123 still passes by the place where the old railroad station used to be, and from which I left for El Paso and college. The train no longer stops in Seguin; one only hears it speed by. It seems that progress, budgets, and efficient freeways have made train service in Seguin a thing of the past. Anyone wishing to travel by train today must go to the station in San Antonio. But in my memory, the old railroad station in Seguin is still there, and I can still see my father, mother, siblings, and cousins there waiting with me before I boarded the train that would take me away.

One block beyond where the railroad station once stood is the place where my uncle Beto tried his hand at running a restaurant. I think the name of that restaurant was El Azteca. It did not work out for my uncle, but it was fun while it lasted. We still have an old photograph of the day the restaurant opened and was blessed by Eugenio Vidaurri, the minister. It was not long after that that my uncle moved away from Seguin to try another project somewhere else.

Farther down Austin Street is the big old Victorian house where I took piano lessons for a few months; but I quit because I did not think it was the thing for a boy to do. I felt like I was the only Chicanito in South Central Texas taking piano lessons. All of my sisters had taken or were taking piano lessons, and it was assumed that I would do the same. My mother made the arrangements with Mrs. Bertha Ayres, the piano teacher, and I obediently set out to learn to play. I was a miserable failure at the keyboards. To get to the lessons every week, I had to walk from the barrio through the Anglo neighborhood across Guadalupe Street and along Austin Street carrying a large lesson book. The piano lesson book was too big to hide. I was too easy a target. I remember one day a big kid came up to me and scared me to death—I ran to the nearest house and banged on the door. Luckily, no one came to the door, but running to the house was enough to scare off my tormentor. I rushed home, my face wet with tears, and begged to be excused from piano lessons.

Turning west at the First Methodist Church on Krezdorn Street one enters a neighborhood that once was prime Anglo territory; it is now a barrio. I cannot help but think that my uncle Berna helped in this transformation when he moved there several years ago. I remember walking or riding my bike through this neighborhood when I was in junior high. It was my first direct experience of being outside the barrio by myself. I felt somewhat nervous and strangely out of place there. The neatly trimmed yards, paved streets, and new cars parked in the driveways were quite a contrast to the barrio across Guadalupe Street where I lived.

Four or five blocks beyond this neighborhood is Guadalupe Street, where I was born and reared. When I reach Guadalupe Street, the home of my Papagrande and Mamagrande greets me as my birthplace. Right next door is my parents' house, where I spent the first seventeen years of my life. When my parents and grandparents bought the residential lot, all the other lots in the area, with the exception of the Burgers' lot next door, were owned by Mexicans. But the Burgers quickly sold to Mr. Bailey, an old black gentleman who built what seemed like a never-ending series of pens for his goats and cow. The gravel pit that had been part of our backyard later became part of the city dump and landfill.

Seguin is home, and every time I return to Seguin I am home, back to the place and people I remember. Each block and street holds memories. I see myself climbing the trees in the backyard, playing with my cousins Tin and Gerito in the gravel pit behind our house, and walking to Juan N. Seguin Elementary School. I imagine riding my bike to school, sweeping the sidewalk of Seguin Leader Department Store, and attending the funerals of my father and grandparents.

It is said that you can never go back home. These reflections are not attempts to return to Seguin or to go home again. The Seguin that I experienced and remember is not there anymore. Seguin has changed; downtown is a ghost of the past. People I do not know populate Guadalupe Street. Our house at 802 North Guadalupe is seeing its last days. The old gravel pit has been filled and paved over. The schools are integrated, and Seguin Leader Department Store is no more. When I visit the church, I recognize only the few remaining older members of the congregation. My *abuelitos* died many years ago. Don Adolfo, Isaac Garza, and El Apache have been dead for years. Now only memories survive. However, this does not diminish Seguin's importance in my life. Seguin is very much alive in me. It is real and an important part of my development. But it is not simply roots from the past, a time and place remembered. Seguin is a part of my self with whom I am in constant conversation and debate. Seguin represents the foundation of my ethnic and religious identity.

Latino and Protestant

Seguin grounded me in two very important sources of identity—ethnicity and religious identity. I am both Mexican-American and Protestant. Being a Mexican-American and a Protestant emerged as profoundly significant life experiences and aspects of my self-understanding as well as my understanding of the world around me. I was a Latino in an Anglo world and a Protestant in a Catholic barrio. As a Latino in an Anglo world, I belonged to a segment of society that was viewed as marginal and insignificant with regard to the mainstream. We were different because of our ethnicity and culture, and thus subjected to prejudice, discrimination, and segregation.

In the Mexican-American barrio, we were different because we were Protestant. Our religious identity and lifestyle separated us in many ways from other Latinos and subjected us to both anti-Protestant and anti-Catholic attitudes and behavior. Both our ethnicity and our religious identity distinguished and separated us within the two communities that formed our world and thus shaped our life experience and worldview. We lived in both worlds and yet did not fully belong to either.

To some extent, we developed our own socioreligious community. This community was centered on the church. Church activities served as an alternative to social activities in the broader public arena. Thus, the church made every effort to provide its members with a wide array of opportunities. Because we could not attend dances or go to movies, but needed a social life, especially opportunities for boys to meet girls and vice versa, the church made sure that there were sufficient youth activities to keep us occupied with weekly recreational events, summer camp, regional conferences, and vacation Bible school.

For adults, the church provided organized activities for the women as well as for the men. *La Sociedad Feminil* (the Women's Society) and *Hombres Metodistas* (Methodist Men) were active church associations. These groups held weekly meetings, engaged in fund-raising like selling tamales to the public, maintained the church property, and sponsored covered dish meals. *Compadrazgo* systems were primarily within the church family, and church peers usually made up the primary friendship circle. In essence, Hispanic Protestants developed an alternative social system grounded on Protestant values and lifestyles. Such an alternative religious and social system profoundly shaped our lives, our worldview, and our self-understanding. However, it also isolated us from the rest of the world.

I was thoroughly Mexican as well. Segregated Seguin provided social structures that were overtly based on ethnicity and race. Families, neighborhoods, schools, and even churches were organized along racial and ethnic lines. I am a product of such a segregated society. Thus, as a Mexican-American, I spent my early years, especially from birth through elementary school age, in family, neighborhood, and school settings that were thoroughly Mexican-American. Our language, lifestyles, and identities were Mexican-American. We understood ourselves to be Mexican-American, and the external environment told us this was so. My early childhood was Mexican.

I was taught the rules and expectations of a segregated society, as well as the price for breaking those rules. I learned that I was Mexican-American, or "Mexican," and as such I followed a certain social track. I was born and reared on Guadalupe Street, did not speak English until I entered school at the age of six, attended the Mexican elementary school and a Spanish-language church, and lived within a Mexican cultural context. I was probably considered a good Mexican because I did not break most social rules. There was one expectation I did not fulfill: I succeeded academically and graduated from high school.

Such an environment drilled in me that my race and ethnicity were at the core of who I was. The town of Seguin, like most of the United States during the pre-civil rights era, was an excellent environment for learning about the significance of race and ethnicity. Its social structures, institutions, and public life were clearly based on race and ethnicity. I learned in which part of town I belonged, which schools I could attend, and which church would welcome me. The media reported the race or ethnicity of individuals as something the reader needed to know. It defined me as a "Mexican" and taught me that my culture and ethnicity were important, though usually not for the right reasons. To a large extent, this definition was imposed from the outside. It was not what we claimed to be, or how we saw each other and ourselves, but rather how the dominant, Anglo population saw and defined us. In essence, Seguin defined me and thus contributed to my self-identity. As a result, my self-identity consists of a strong dose of ethnic identity informed by a racially and ethnically structured society.

There were other important influences in my ethnic formation.

These were internal, from within the family and community, and reflected more positive notions of ethnic culture and identity, nurturing and natural notions that reflected the self-understanding shared by the ethnic community. My family and community taught me that I was a Mexican-American and that this was important, but their lessons were different from those I learned outside. They taught me that the joys of family, the value of *respeto*, and the celebration of life through food, music, and humor were Mexican. I learned to know God and to see the world through a deep sense of spirituality, mystery, and awe.

I learned culture from my parents, grandparents, and extended family. They taught me Spanish as my first language, and they nurtured me in a cultural context rich in familial relationships and caring. I grew up surrounded with the colors, sounds, and aromas of the Mexican culture. I heard the stories of my ancestors and was instructed in key values. But most of all, I learned by watching and observing how my parents and extended family carried out their daily lives in a spirit of family and community. They taught me that we were Mexican-American, and I learned what that meant by studying their lives.

But we were also American. We were products of an American social and educational system that shaped and molded our self-understanding. We rejected the notion that we were foreigners. Seguin was our home; our men served our nation in the military and went to war. We claimed our citizenship with pride and embraced English as one of our languages. To a larger extent, we bought into the notion of the Protestant work ethic and engaged in serious study and dutiful employment. Mexican-Americans understood themselves to be American. I grew up with the clear understanding that I was an American.

After graduating from Juan N. Seguin Elementary School, Mexican-Americans were sent to Anglo-dominated schools across Guadalupe Street. Our social and ethnic isolation ended. We were introduced to an entirely new and different culture, including language, values, rules, and goals. To survive we had to learn Anglo rules. To succeed we had to master those rules. This resulted in our acculturation. We became Mexican-*Americans* in the cultural sense of the term. We were no longer living exclusively according to the language, values, and culture of our homes and *abuelitos,* but instead we had to actively develop social and cultural skills to maneuver in an Anglo world. To some extent, we learned the Anglo ways. My generation became the bridge between those living in ethnic isolation and those who became more fully acculturated. To a large extent, we became the bicultural generation of Mexican-Americans.

With regard to my religious life and upbringing, my childhood and youth were strongly centered in the church. My parents and grandparents were devoted to La Trinidad Iglesia Metodista. Our family had identified strongly with that congregation and religious tradition since the founding of the church. The ministers were frequent visitors in our home. They were there for coffee, meals, planning programs for the church, or prayer. The church was our second home. Our weekly routine and annual activities centered on church events. Going to church was second nature to us. La Trinidad Iglesia Metodista was our church.

I learned about God in my mother's arms. My grandmother introduced me to the Bible, *coritos,* and prayer. Her spirituality nurtured and shaped us. The faith of our parents guided our home life. We lived a religious life as if that was the only way to live. As a young child, my religious training and formation was a joint effort by the church and the family, including our grandmother Molina.

Just as my early ethnic formation took place in cultural isolation, my religious formation took place in religious isolation. My entire extended family belonged to the same church. Thus, I was not exposed to any other form of religious expression or tradition as a young child. I have no recollection of visiting another church, especially the Catholic church. I did not know anything about denominations or other churches. When I saw other churches, I assumed that they were like ours.

The faith of my family was Protestant. I learned that religious faith was grounded in the Bible and in personally and directly knowing God. To be a Christian was to be pietistic and hard-working. This meant avoiding the "ways of the world," such as smoking, drinking alcohol, dancing, and going to the movie theaters. The spiritual disciplines of prayer, meditation, and Bible study were essential and to be supported by regular attendance at church services and activities. A good Christian was a good church person.

However, religious isolation could not last very long in the barrio. Venturing out to public school exposed me to other children from other religious traditions. I quickly came to learn about Catholics when the priest tried to recruit me for *doctrina*. I was not Catholic. I was Protestant. Thus, beginning with my first year of school. I was introduced to the Catholic/Protestant reality.

My religious experience and identity were shaped by the anti-Catholic and anti-Protestant realities in Seguin of the 1940s and 1950s. The Catholic and Protestant worlds were separate. You had to decide to which you belonged and in which you would live. Both sides demanded loyalty. You could not participate in both. You had to choose sides. To choose one was always viewed as having left the other behind, and that involved losing friends and relationships.

Latino Protestants and Catholics did not merely coexist, they actually lived in constant tension, conflict, and a certain animosity that touched various aspects of my daily life and relationships and in turn shaped my own identity. It was impossible to avoid such tensions if you were a Protestant Mexican-American living in the barrio. I lived in a world in which religion and religious faith were of crucial importance, yet I was subjected to religious animosity because of the religious tradition with which I identified. Externally, I confronted anti-Protestantism; internally, I learned anti-Catholicism.

The external forces of anti-Protestantism, which I experienced in Seguin, were manifested in many ways but especially in attitudes and perceptions about Protestants. We were untouchables. Catholics were convinced that to be Protestant was to be anti-

Catholic. We were the enemy. We were out to make Protestants out of Catholics by preaching erroneous things about the Catholic tradition, especially about saints, the Virgin Mary, and the pope. Thus Catholic homes had to be protected from Protestant propaganda by tacking anti-Protestant warnings on doors and windows.

Internally, I also learned anti-Catholicism. I was taught that Catholics indeed worshipped false idols (saints), worshipped Mary as the mother of God, and were loyal to Rome and to the pope above all other authority. All of this was supposedly because the Catholic faith was not biblical and Catholics were ignorant of the Bible. Besides, Catholics lived unholy lives—they smoked, drank alcohol, and danced. The Catholic belief and practice of confession was an easy way to sin, be forgiven, and sin again.

On the other hand, as Protestants we were taught that we had a superior religious understanding and lifestyle. First of all, we believed in the Bible, and our loyalty and faith were totally committed to God through Jesus Christ. We were taught that we did not need mediators such as Mary and the saints, who were merely human and without divine powers. As Protestants, we were taught that we were right and that Catholics were wrong. Conversion from Catholicism to Protestantism was interpreted as a step toward salvation. To be Protestant was to be Christian; to be Catholic was to be idolatrous.

It was assumed then, as it is now, that to be Hispanic was to be Catholic. Being Latino and Protestant was perceived as a contradiction. How could you be Mexican-American and not be Catholic? Certainly, you must have turned your back on the Catholic Church and the faith of your people. My early experience in Seguin involved many personal confrontations and challenges to my religious identity. Yet those questions puzzled me. I never converted from Roman Catholicism to Protestantism. I was a fourth-generation Methodist and Protestant. I never felt that I had betrayed the Catholic Church or my forefathers; they were all Protestant, too. Papá Luis, Mamadita, the Maldonados, the Molinas, and the Gallardos were all Protestant. They were leaders in La

Trinidad Iglesia Metodista. My parents themselves were reared in the church and met there. So, as a youngster, I assumed that I was quite normal, and I was quite content with my family, my ethnicity, my religious identity, and myself.

It was the questioning of my religious identity, the increasing reminders that I was different, and especially the social price that I and many around me paid because of our religious faith, that left their mark on me and made that identity even more important to me. My Protestant family and friends paid a price for their religious beliefs and identity. I became increasingly aware that I was a Protestant in a Catholic community, which made it a point to tell me so and to question my authenticity. The questioning, the attitudes toward our church, signs against Protestants, shunning, and family rifts, all contributed to the reinforcement of religious identity as important in my self-understanding.

Seguin was no different from most other communities in Texas or in the Southwest at that time. Protestant Latinos experienced similar dynamics in New Mexico, Colorado, and California. It is part of being Latino and Protestant, and it is a significant element of our self-identities. Latino Protestants find it very difficult not to include religious identity as a central part of their self-identity because of the significant role it has played in their formative experiences.

Although the religious climate has changed since Vatican II and there have been many ecumenical gains during the last two decades, many Latino communities, families, and individuals unfortunately continue to be torn because of religious identity. Anti-Catholic and anti-Protestant attitudes linger and continue to shape life in barrios and Latino communities today, especially in small towns. We still do not know what impact recent immigration from Mexico and other Latin American nations will have on Protestant-Catholic relations in this country. Many new immigrants are coming as Protestants and many others as Catholic. They bring diverse religious experiences, especially with regard to Catholic-Protestant relations. Many of these experiences are not positive.

However, there are hopeful signs. Protestant and Catholic theologians are engaged in fruitful dialogue and increasingly share experiences. Even among some lay groups there have been breakthroughs in communication. The fact that my sister Amelia befriended the Catholic priest and played the organ at the Catholic church is a tremendous breakthrough in Seguin. It is hoped that these signs will contribute to more mutual understanding and respect between Latino Protestants and Catholics.

To be Hispanic and Protestant of the generation reared before the civil rights movement, the Chicano Movement, and Vatican II means to have experienced both overt racism and religious prejudice. Such attitudes led to racial segregation and religious divisions. Ethnic intolerance and religious divisions profoundly influenced this generation of Mexican-Americans. Such ethnic and religious attitudes led to the development of alternative systems of social life and religious communities that deeply influenced and shaped Mexican-American Protestants. It is no wonder that for Hispanic Protestants, ethnicity and religious identity are central to their self- and group identities.

Closing Thoughts

Now that I have made the full circle back to Seguin, I have discovered what I had known from the very beginning. I value my family, my ethnic culture, and membership in the Hispanic community and the church, especially the Hispanic church. And just as family, church, and community were the powerful forces in my life experience in the past, today they are equally important. Yesterday, they were forces that shaped my life. Today, they serve more as motivators and sources of joy, and in that sense they continue to shape my life.

My family—my wife, Charlotte, our two sons, David III and Carlos, our daughter-in-law, Kecia, and our granddaughters, Maya and Rayna—are central to my life today, and there is very little I would not do for them. As an adult, a parent, and now a grandparent, I find myself thinking about my parents and grandparents. I find assurance, strength, and motivation in their memory. When I am surrounded by my family, whether it is at Thanksgiving, a birthday celebration, Christmas, or any other day of the year, my thoughts drift back and I imagine that my parents probably felt as good and as satisfied as I do at that very moment. In a sense I find myself conversing with them, sharing the moment with them. When our first granddaughter, Maya, was born, David III called to give us the good news. In the midst of his joy, David said, "I finally know how much you loved me." Our son discovered what love for a child means, and in his love for his infant child he discovered how much we loved him. I now know how much my *abuelitos* and parents loved me and how important the family was for them. It is with a sense of obligation and gratitude to them that I approach being a parent and a grandparent today. I owe it to those who loved me. I am merely passing on the love of family to the next generation. It is they who have formed who I am today.

As I revisit the realities of my hometown of the 1940s and 1950s, I am reminded that although much has changed, much continues to be the same. The story of economic and political marginality has changed only slightly for the Mexican-American population. Unfortunately, for too many Latinos, poverty continues to be a daily struggle. Culture and language are now a public debate. When I was a child fifty years ago, teachers told us not to speak Spanish; today some legislators and organized movements would like to outlaw it. And certainly, racism has not been eradicated from public life and personal attitudes. We are still fighting the war against racial prejudice and institutional racism. Although our numbers suggest increasing economic and political impact, we are still viewed as insignificant, a "minority" culture, and foreign. The pain and injustices that I saw in my return to Seguin are just as painful. The price that my community paid to survive so that I could reach today is a reality I cannot forget. I owe it to them to continue.

My journey back to Seguin has equally reaffirmed my sense of culture and ethnic identity. Although today I call myself a Tejano, I was reared as a Mexican and then as a Mexican-American. But whatever term we use, at the core is a shared sense of peoplehood, history, and social experience. Culture involves sharing a common language, values, worldview, and the many products of a common social life. I am reminded that I share these and many other cultural realities with the people who call themselves Mexican, Mexican-American, Chicano, Hispanic, Latino, or Tejano. I am able to affirm my identity and personal pleasure in things and experiences we call Mexican or Hispanic.

La Trinidad Iglesia Metodista in Seguin continues to serve as a center of religious and social life for Mexican-American Protestants in my hometown. It serves as both a social and a religious center for its members, and in this regard it is duplicated throughout the United States, especially in large urban areas with substantial Hispanic populations. My sense is that all such churches continue to serve the same purpose—to provide religious and social centers of life for Hispanic Protestants. Why do Latino churches still exist in the post-civil rights era? Probably for the same reasons they existed when I was a child. Today's society is also segregated in its housing, educational, social, and religious structures. Racial attitudes still exist and contribute to separation. Hispanics continue to desire to worship and celebrate their faith in their own language and culture. As a product of a Mexican-American church, I continue to worship in a Hispanic church.

The trip back to Seguin also reminded me of great pain. I was reminded that as Latino Christians we were divided; we were either Catholics or Protestants. The more I think about it, the more I am convinced that this division was imposed and maintained by clergy outsiders to the Latino community who placed institutional self-interest above the life of the community. These were Anglo Protestant missionaries and European Catholic priests. For example, Anglo Protestant missionaries wanted to make good Protestants out of Mexicans-Americans. To them this meant we should become pietistic Americans with a strong Protestant work ethic. It also meant that we should turn our backs on anything and everything Catholic or Mexican. To convert was to become anti-Catholic and to drop out of the barrio's social life. European Catholic priests came into our communities and painted Protestants as heretics, traitors, and threats to Catholicism. Thus, good Catholics were to avoid all Protestants. And so our community was split. Revisiting the religious realities of my childhood has helped me to recognize my own learned religious prejudices and biases. I must recognize these prejudices, but this does not mean that I must accept or maintain them. On the contrary, because I am aware of them now, I must make every effort to reach across religious barriers that separated us for so long.

Today, I seek to better understand the Catholic tradition. I have visited the Vatican and the shrine of the Virgin of Guadalupe in Mexico City several times and have attended Mass. I have participated in Catholic religious activities during Holy Week, including marching with Penitentes and participating in Morada services. I have done the twelve Stations of the Cross. I have spoken with my Catholic brothers and sisters in an effort to understand but also to rid myself of the anti-Catholic and anti-Protestant baggage that I have carried since childhood.

Why should I be religious in today's secular society? Why should I invest my time and energy teaching in a school of theology? My personal trip back to Seguin has also taken me back to spiritual roots and sources that still nourish me. Remembering my grandparents' faith and prayers, recalling them reading their Bibles, hearing their songs through the ears of memory, and revisiting the small *iglesia* have reestablished a connection to my spiritual beginnings. It is not that I had forgotten them or lost them along the way. It is more of a reminder that what I have today is a gift and a trust from my spiritual ancestors. I value that spirituality and owe it to them to nourish and pass it on to the next generation.

I learned that I am the recipient of a rich cultural and spiritual heritage that nourishes and strengthens me as I confront the challenges of today. I am indebted to my family, my spiritual teachers, and my barrio for their instruction and contributions to my life. Their spirituality and religious faith have shaped my life and vocation. They passed on a culture and an ethnic identity that I celebrate. I have learned that I value who I am, maybe because of the very pain suffered by those who formed me. Because of them, I can claim that I am Mexican-American and Protestant.

❋

My journey after Seguin took me to the U.S.-Mexico border, where I studied at Texas Western College (now the University of Texas at El Paso) from 1961 to 1965. I became fascinated with Mexican history and majored in history. Moving from Seguin to El Paso was a social and cultural shock. I went from a small Texas town to a major border city, from a town in which we were in the ethnic minority to a city where Mexicans were the majority and dominant population. It offered an incredible affirmation of culture, ethnic identity, and self-esteem. In addition, it confirmed that I was an American citizen and not from Mexico, an important fact in crossing the border.

From El Paso, my bride, Charlotte, and I moved on to Dallas, where I studied theology at Southern Methodist University (SMU). This was another major life transition. I moved from a Mexican border town to a major corporate city in which Hispanics were truly in the minority in 1965. In addition, SMU was an educational center where the wealthy sent their young to be properly educated. My wife and I lived in a dorm for married students. For the first time, I felt I had Anglo peers. Between academic years I worked in the antipoverty program in western Kansas serving Mexican farmworkers. This experience gave me renewed insights into the oppressed conditions of farmworkers. I developed a sense of outrage in Kansas. At SMU, I learned a sense of social justice.

After SMU, I served as a minister in Fort Worth and became so involved in the Chicano Movement that the Fort Worth Metropolitan Board of Missions hired me as a full-time urban minister. I was involved in community organization and social services in an urban setting. I was convinced that I was doing what was needed. Justice ministries were my calling. But I was not prepared in social analysis and social action. An opportunity opened up to study at the University of California. I immediately gave up my position, and we headed to Berkeley, where I received a master's degree in social work and a doctoral degree. I went on to teach for ten years at the Graduate School of Social Work at the University of Texas at Arlington. For the next sixteen years I taught at the Perkins School of Theology at Southern Methodist University. Now I am president of the Iliff School of Theology in Denver.

I never thought that I would have an academic career, especially not in a school of theology. My father never quite understood or believed what I did to earn a living. Reading books and teaching a class twice a week was not work in his view, and certainly not worth the salary I was receiving. My mother still asks me about my hours and workdays. It has been an incredible journey. My father's generation worked with their hands; I work with my mind. They worked in the sun; I work in an office. They could not ask questions; asking questions is part of my job. They were called "hands"; I am called "President Maldonado."

I do not accept these differences as a personal reward. On the contrary, it was precisely because of the hard work and dreams of my parents and others that I am able to do what I do today. Thus, I have an obligation to tell our story and to share with the next generation the history of those who have gone before them. By telling my story, I am telling the story of our ancestors and challenging them to learn from our experiences.